Born Againism

PERSPECTIVES ON A MOVEMENT

Born Againism

ERIC W. GRITSCH

FORTRESS PRESS   Philadelphia

Library of Congress Cataloging in Publication Data

Gritsch, Eric W.
  Born-againism, perspectives on a movement.

  Bibliography: p.
  1. Conversion—History of doctrines. 2. Millennialism
—History. 3. Fundamentalism—History. 4. Pentecostalism
—History. I. Title.
BT780.G74   270.8   81-70595
ISBN 0-8006-1625-1   AACR2

9399L81 Printed in the United States of America 1-1625

"I saw a new heaven and a new earth . . ." (Rev. 21:1).

"All scripture is inspired by God . . ." (2 Tim. 3:16).

"There are different kinds of spiritual gifts, but the same spirit gives them" (1 Cor. 12:4 TEV).

Jesus told Nicodemus: "unless one is born anew, he cannot see the kingdom of God" (John 3:3).

Contents

Contents

Introduction

What does it mean to be "born again"? Defenders and critics of a "born-again movement," the news media, and religious revivalists provide a confusing variety of answers. You are born again when you (1) are baptized—as an infant, a second time as a believing adult, or without water and solely by the Holy Spirit; (2) have a traumatic conversion experience, speak in tongues, or change your life from one of egotism to one of sacrificial love for others; (3) believe that the Bible contains inspired and inerrant divine truth, reject "unbiblical" truths such as Charles Darwin's theory of evolution, or uphold monogamy and oppose polygamy; (4) expect the imminent end of the world, affirm the secret rapture of true believers before the Last Judgment, or discern your own time as the last thousand years of human history; (5) become a member of a moral majority defending the puritan ethic of marital sex, free enterprise in business, and public prayer in schools; or (6) hold that the United States has been called by God to be the defender of Christian ideals in an unchristian world, or join an ideological crusade against godless Communism. The list of answers could easily be expanded.

Are these and other answers enough to create a born-again movement? And if so, what are the principal affirmations holding such a movement together? This book tries to show that there is a born-again movement which has discernible historical roots and which is held together by a relentless quest for membership in the "kingdom of God." At the center of the movement is what might be called "the Nicodemus factor," referring to the rather mysterious encounter between Jesus and Nicodemus recorded in the Gospel of John (3:1–21). Curious about Jesus' power as "a teacher come from

God," the Pharisee and respected political leader Nicodemus is confronted with the assertions that "unless one is born anew [from above], he cannot see the kingdom of God" and "unless one is born of water and the Spirit, he cannot enter the kingdom of God." In addition, Nicodemus is treated to a lengthy homily on the relationship between God's promises to Israel and their fulfillment through the coming of the Son of God so "that the world might be saved through him."

The story is told with an eye on the popular myth of the redemption of the world through the disclosure of "secret knowledge" (*gnosis*). Many intellectuals of the Greco-Roman world were attracted to this myth, which promised the coming of a "figure of light" who would initiate a cadre of disciples, taking them out of their exile in darkness to a new, bright world of salvation.

There were numerous versions of the myth, but the Gospel of John used it to make the decisive point that Christ is the only path from the darkness of sin into the light of redemption. This journey is accomplished only by way of an existential encounter with the man Jesus rather than through any sophisticated philosophical procedure. Jesus is the embodied "Word" (*logos*), who was with God from the beginning and is the "true light" become flesh (John 1:14). Extraordinary power and "glory" (*doxa*) are revealed in the words and deeds of Jesus, who changes water into wine at a wedding (John 2:1–11) and raises a buried corpse from the dead (John 11:1–44). The Gospel of John always links Jesus to God ("No one comes to the Father, but by me," John 14:6) and to the Holy Spirit ("whom the Father will send in my name," John 14:26). Conversion is linked to baptism (rebirth is by "water and the Spirit," John 3:5). Baptism leads to a life of sacrificial love ("that a man lay down his life for his friends," John 15:13). This, then, is the context in which Jesus told Nicodemus that "unless one is born anew, he cannot see the kingdom of God" (John 3:3).

This passage clearly indicates that Christian life has origins different from biological life. Christian life begins with penance, that is, "a change of mind" (*metanoia*). On another occasion Jesus said that people must "turn and become like children" in order to enter the kingdom of God (Matt. 18:3). Once a person is conceived and "born from above," that person is put into the new relationship of "faith from below," as John 3:1–8 and 3:9–21 indicate. A decisive shift has occurred in one's life—the result of the encounter between God, who comes as the force of light through Christ, and the world, which lives in the darkness of sin. This new relationship encompasses the judgment that "no one born of God commits sin" (1 John 3:9); it is the new reality begun through Christ, water, and the Holy Spirit which will lead to the end depicted in apocalyptic language in the Revelation of John. The first Christians could therefore say, "we have been born anew to a living hope through the resurrection of Jesus Christ from the dead, and to an inheritance which is imperishable . . ." (1 Pet. 1:3–4). To be baptized into the death and resurrection of Jesus is "the washing of regeneration and renewal in the Holy Spirit" (Titus 3:5).

Being born anew is not a statement of objective fact, as if the encounter with Christ through water and Spirit guaranteed sinlessness. Rather, it is a statement of faith which clings to the promise that having become a child of God, one will attain eternal adulthood with God when God transforms this world into a new creation. "We are God's children now; it does not yet appear what we shall be, but we know that when he appears we shall be like him" (1 John 3:2).

Although all of Christian life could be called a born-again movement, the Nicodemus factor has shaped some Christians in a particular way. There is good evidence that what has been called the born-again movement in the United States is rooted in a revival of the millennial hope that existed in England in the 1790s at the time of the French Revolution, and that the quest to be born again is expressed in affirmations which are shaped by what has been dubbed "fundamentalism" and "pentecostalism," also called the "holiness revival" or "charismatic" movement. This book tells the story of fundamentalism and the charismatic movement, beginning with a sketch of their historical roots in the revival of millennial hope in England and the United States. A view of the born-again phenomenon in historical perspective is direly needed in order to arrive at a balanced judgment of what it means to be born again.

While this treatment of the born-again movement may seem too limited to readers who are looking for original research and a theological stance different from mine, I nevertheless hope to challenge them and all readers to begin an encounter with the born-again movement through this book. Such an encounter may demonstrate the principal value of ecumenical dialogue, namely, that a person learns more about his or her own tradition in the process of carefully and critically encountering other traditions. The born-again movement challenges ecumenical Christianity in a variety of ways. To recognize this, to study the movement, and to engage in dialogue with it whenever possible are the main tasks of a teaching ministry concerned with the ecumenical dimensions of Christian pluralism.

All biblical quotations in this book are from the Revised Standard Version. The selected, annotated readings listed at the back of the book are intended to encourage readers to continue their education in this important area of contemporary religious life.

I am grateful to my former colleague and friend, Joseph A. Burgess, for encouraging me to write this book, and to colleagues Robert W. Jenson and Christa Ressmeyer Klein for providing helpful suggestions. My spouse, Ruth, deserves special thanks for editorial advice and typing.

EWG

1

A Revival of Millennial Hope

SPECULATIONS ABOUT THE END TIME

Christian hope is concentrated in the plea, "Come, Lord Jesus!" (Rev. 22:20). Such hope looks for liberation from a world come of age and anticipates the kingdom which will commence with Christ's Second Coming. Cataclysmic events, natural disasters, and violent historical constellations have always intensified this hope.

The speculation regarding the possible time and method with which this hope will be fulfilled is called apocalypticism. Biblical apocalypticism (*apokalypsis*, meaning "revelation"), which is explicit in such writings as Daniel and Revelation, focused on the advent of a Messiah who would usher in an everlasting kingdom. A powerful component of apocalypticism is the doctrine concerning a final age of one thousand years—a millennium. Its Christian formulation is linked to prophecies of a final battle between angelic forces and Satan, depicted as a dragonlike beast. Satan will be "bound . . . for a thousand years that he should deceive the nations no more, till the thousand years are ended. After that he must be loosed for a little while" (Rev. 20:2–3).

The North African bishop Augustine linked these biblical prophecies with a new notion of time that had a beginning (creation), a center (Christ), and an end (Christ's Second Coming). This concept of time was quite different from that of Greek philosophy, which viewed time as cyclical, that is, without a distinct past, present, or future. Augustine envisioned time and history as the struggle between the "city of God" (the title of his major work, written between A.D. 413 and A.D. 426) and the "city of the devil." According to this vision, the category of time has priority over the category of thought. Augustine argued that time is not just a con-

13

cept, but a reality which cannot be controlled by thinking. Human beings and their immortal souls are placed within time to be tested in the struggle between the love of self (pride) and the love of God (humility). Thus all of life is a pilgrimage in time marked by constant conflict between good and evil, God and Satan, and love of self and love for others until the return of Christ at the end of time. The Greek metaphysical ideal of the ultimately good and beautiful was embodied in time in the man Jesus, who gave meaning to the struggle of life. Christ's "body," the church, is the community which discloses God's plan for humankind: the return to a neverending fellowship between creature and Creator.

Augustine thus discerned God as the one who reveals the Deity more in events than in ideas.[1] Disciples of Augustine combined his notion of the struggle between the city of God and the city of the devil with schemes about the end of history. Between 1143 and 1146, for example, the German bishop Otto of Freising wrote a "history of the world," arguing that there are seven periods of world history just as there are seven days of creation. Assuming that his own time was the "sixth day," he anticipated the imminent end of the world, thus becoming the most significant forerunner of those who described the seventh period of world history as the "millennium," the culmination of the struggle between good and evil.

The Italian Cistercian abbott Joachim of Floris understood the thousand years as the period between Christ's ascension and his Second Coming, a time of tribulation. Joachim, who died around 1200, based his speculations about the end time on the year-equals-day theory: "with the Lord one day is as a thousand years, and a thousand years as one day" (2 Pet. 3:8; Ps. 90:4). Daniel 7 and Revelation 13 provided the biblical basis for his scheme: after four empires, symbolized by four animals, the little horn , which grew from the ten horns of the fourth animal, would be the final ruler and would "wear out the saints of the Most High, and . . . think to change the times and the law" (Dan. 7:25). The evil, dragonlike beast with ten horns in Revelation 13 would be allowed to exercise authority for forty-two months (13:5). Accordingly, the promised millennium, a final age of purification, "the age of the Holy Spirit" following the ages of the Father and of the Son, would begin in A.D. 1260.[2]

Millennialists exhibit a fascinating combination of biblical literalism and rationalistic pragmatism. Biblical chronology and numerology are taken literally, though with a peculiar use of time in which all of time unfolds in periods called "covenants" (between God and people) or "dispensations," divinely appointed ages (from *dispensatio*, "arrangement"), which climax in a "golden age" or millennium. Possible contradictions between biblical texts are thereby avoided in order to achieve a meaningful interpretation of the Bible as a whole. Underlying such an interpretation is the ancient scheme of "salvation history"—the understanding of divine revelation and action as "prophecy" (Old Testament) and "fulfillment" (New Testament).

Texts about the end time, especially Daniel 7–9, Joel 2, Matthew 24–25, and Revelation 13, play a key role in the millennial scheme of salvation history. Millennialists of all ages generally assume that their own time is the one during which these biblical prophecies will be fulfilled.

Speculations about the millennium also include the expectation that the Holy Spirit will be poured out with great force. "I will pour out my spirit on all flesh; your sons and your daughters shall prophesy, your old men shall dream dreams, and your young men shall see visions" (Joel 2:28). The Holy Spirit is seen as the link between this world and the next. The gifts or fruits of the Holy Spirit imbue Christians with special powers to assist their prophetic ministry, their struggle against disease, and their hope for the resurrection. The early church was convinced that the Holy Spirit is poured out through Jesus, who links believers to a new life by baptism (Titus 3:5–6). Thus the millennialist interpretation of the Bible as a book containing clues to the end time is accompanied by a drive to achieve a holy life beforehand, so that one will be worthy of reception into the everlasting kingdom.

Millennial speculations have frequently been judged to be foolish, especially when the predicted dates of the end of the world turned out to be erroneous. Nevertheless, millennialists have always been a force in the history of Christian revival. They attempt to revive a concern they consider to be disastrously neglected by the body of Christ (the concern for the end time), which keeps Christians alert in a sinful and fallen world. A fellowship bound together by the knowledge of revelation and salvation is born when the heart feels the Holy Spirit and the mind is enlightened by biblical prophecies about the last days. Millennialism combines rationalist doctrines about Christ's Second Coming with experiences of the Holy Spirit, who verifies the truth of biblical doctrines about the end time. Doctrine derived from Scripture becomes linked to the spiritual, existential certainty grounded in the experiencing of the Holy Spirit, and thus salvation is truly "known."

BRITISH PROPHECIES

Millennial speculations were revived in Britain by Puritans such as Thomas Venner and the Fifth Monarchy Men, and by Enlightenment rationalists such as the Salisbury rector, Daniel Whitby. Whereas Venner taught a fanatic doctrine of tribulation before the end, Whitby stressed rational progress and the coming of a golden age of the church as the transition to Christ's millennium.

The real revival of millennialism came in 1789 with the French Revolution and its aftermath. Numerous prophetic studies regarded the 1790s as the last age before the end, filled with the trials and tribulations prophesied in Matthew 24–25. Napoleon's banishment of Pope Pius VI from Rome to France in 1798 and the pope's subsequent death one year later were interpreted as the fulfillment of the prophecy of Revelation 13: the papacy would be permitted to reign for 1,260 years (starting in A.D. 538) and then would die of its "mortal wound" (Rev. 13:3,5).

Anti-Roman Catholic sentiments were combined with a missionary interest in the Jews. Lewis Way, a rich barrister who had become an Anglican priest after a conversion experience, transformed the bankrupt London Society for Promoting Christianity Among the Jews into an advocate of Protestant Zionism, which attempted to restore Israel in Palestine by resettling dispersed European Jews. By 1825, however, Way's stubborn insistence that Christ would return before the advent of the millennium turned the "Jews Society," as the organization was popularly known, into a failure. Nevertheless, his studies of biblical prophecies, written under the pseudonym Basilicus, became popular in various segments of British society.

The Scottish preacher Edward Irving created the most widespread millennialist fervor in Britain during the 1820s and 1830s.

His sermons, tracts, and conferences attracted many of the rich and the noble to anti-Roman Catholicism and to mission to the Jews, and led to the establishment of a "free," non-Anglican, Irvingian congregation. One convert to Irving's cause, a banker and member of the House of Commons named Henry Drummond, sponsored prophetic conferences at Albury. The 1829 Albury Conference created the first six-point platform of the British millennialists. It stated that (1) the present age or "dispensation" (divinely ordained age) will end with the destruction of the institutional church; (2) Israel will be restored in Palestine; (3) the judgment of God will fall principally on Christendom; (4) the millennium will begin after the judgment; (5) the Second Coming of Christ will occur before the millennium; and (6) the 1,260 years, calculated from Daniel 7 and Revelation 13, began with the establishment of institutional Christendom by Justinian I (who created the first "canon laws") in A.D. 530, and ended with the French Revolution in 1790. The Second Coming of Christ would occur soon afterwards.

Periodicals such as *The Morning Watch, The Christian Herald*, and *The Investigator* created a fervent millennialist climate throughout the British Isles. When people began to "speak in tongues" during a church service in Irving's London congregation, many people regarded the event as the beginning of the end marked by the outpouring of the Holy Spirit. Prophets of doom and charismatic healers joined forces in what was now called the restoration of the Catholic Apostolic Church.

When Irving died in 1834, his crusade against the evils of the established church was continued by the Plymouth Brethren and John Nelson Darby who, in Ireland, had been proclaiming the imminent end of the world since the 1820s. Darby, an Anglican priest deeply disappointed by the politics of the Church of England, at first joined and then led the Brethren. He gradually reached the conviction that all visible churches, whether state or dissenting churches, were dominated by political "systems" rather than by the truth of Scripture. He propagated these views in speeches during many trips to Britain, to the continent, and to the United States, which he visited seven times between 1826 and 1877. Two distinctive features of Darby's theology caused debates among the Plymouth Brethren: the doctrine of the "secret rapture" or the

17

"any-moment coming of Christ," and his interpretation of Scripture as the source of both Jewish and Christian truths, even though the two have little in common.

Darby's doctrine of the "secret rapture" asserts that the true believers—the invisible, spiritual fellowship of Christians throughout the world—will be lifted up (raptured) to Christ with no warnings or suffering beforehand. There is some evidence for this assertion in Matt. 24:36–44, which depicts the Flood at the time of Noah and the Second Coming of Christ as sudden events. "Then two men will be in the field; one is taken and one is left. Two women will be grinding at the mill; one is taken and one is left.... Therefore you also must be ready; for the Son of man is coming at an hour you do not expect." Darby stressed that this rapture or carrying off could come at any moment and would be secret.

Opposition to this doctrine was led by Benjamin Wills Newton, an Oxford Fellow who had joined the Plymouth Brethren in 1831. Newton argued that the Bible neither taught such a doctrine of rapture nor prophesied a secret Second Coming of Christ. Instead, he insisted that Christ's Second Coming would be preceded by certain events and tribulations such as Peter's death (John 21:18–19), that believers and unbelievers would be separated at the end time, (indicated by the parable of the wheat and the weeds, Matt. 13:24–30), and that Scripture therefore refutes a doctrine of secret rapture.

Darby countered these arguments with the thesis that there are two Scriptures, as it were, one for Christians and one for Jews; that the tribulation texts (Matthew 24–25, for example) apply only to the Jews; and that the final "dispensation," the age of the church from Pentecost to the end time, is a mystery whose meaning will be clearly disclosed at the time of the secret rapture when Christians will be lifted up to Christ. After the invisible church "is raptured out of the world," Darby declared, God will again turn to Israel and restore it in Palestine. In the meantime, proper dispensationalist interpreters of Scripture must distinguish between the millennialist Christian truth and the Zionist Jewish truth in Scripture; they must "rightly handle the truth" (2 Tim. 2:15).

By 1849, the Plymouth Brethren had split into two factions, the Open and the Exclusive Brethren. The latter were led by Darby, who accused Newton and his followers of heresy. In the 1860s, the Brethren dispersed all over Europe and began their migration to the United States.

Many Protestants in England and America had by this time become attracted to the Brethren's dispensational millennialism. The features of this millennialism have endured until today: successive dispensations—divinely ordained ages or covenants, climaxing in a premillennial age marked by the apostasy of the established churches and the final gathering of all true Christians through the preaching of the essential Word of God; the rapture or carrying off of the gathered "bride of Christ," the true church; the Second Coming of Christ and the beginning of the millennium, the final age, after the collapse of worldly Christendom. One can still hear today the echo of the Darby–Newton controversy over the question of whether there will be a time of trial and tribulation before the Second Coming of Christ, or whether there will be a secret rapture, swift and without any warning.

THE AMERICAN CONNECTION

There was a natural blend between British millennial hopes and the American dream expressed by the colonists who, in 1776, had achieved independence from Britain. "I really believe," declared Samuel H. Cox in 1846 when he had become moderator of the General Assembly of the Presbyterian Church, "that God has got America within anchorage, and that upon that arena, He intends to display His prodigies for the millennium."[3]

Cox was by no means alone in his expectations. William Miller, a convert from deism to millennialism, predicted the beginning of the millennium for the year 1843. This committed Baptist from Vermont had arrived at his conclusion following calculations based on Daniel 8–9 and on Archbishop Ussher's chronology in the King James Version of the Bible: using the day-equals-year analogy and Ussher's date of 457 B.C. for the events described in Daniel 9, the seventy weeks of Dan. 9:24 added up to A.D. 33, the year of Christ's death; and the 2,300 years of Dan. 8:14 added up to 1843. The well-known Boston preacher, Joshua V. Himes, joined Miller and this millennial scheme was propagated through meetings, tracts, and the hymns from their hymnal, *The Millennial Harp*.

When 1843 passed without millennial incidents, the Millerites established an "adventist" church in Vermont to await the delayed end. By 1855, the group was large enough to establish a headquarters in Battle Creek, Michigan, for the movement now called the Seventh-Day Adventists. By 1868 the Seventh-Day Adventists had received sufficient support from wealthy businessmen such as John H. Kellogg, the king of breakfast cereals, to launch a general conference as the focus of a new denomination.

Millerite and Darbyist millennialism flourished especially in the new American urban centers of New York, Boston, Chicago, and St. Louis. Several millennialist periodicals disseminated prophecies about the end time: the *Millennial Harbinger* of the Disciples of Christ, the Mormon *Millennial Star,* and the independent *Theological and Literary Journal.* Established in 1848 by David Nevins Lord, president of Dartmouth College, the *Theological and Literary Journal* tried to bring order to the confusing prophecies of the various millennial groups.

Most denominations had become involved in one way or another in millennialist speculations by the time of the Civil War. A cadre of intellectuals published an American millennial creed in 1863. The creed appeared in the first issue of the *Prophetic Times,* a monthly periodical edited by Lutheran, Episcopalian, Presbyterian, Dutch Reformed, and Baptist theologians, led by the pastor of the largest English Lutheran church in America, Joseph A. Seiss. Seiss had written books on millennialism, edited the *Lutheran,* and was president of the board of the Lutheran Theological Seminary in Philadelphia from 1865 until his death in 1902.

The American millennial creed consisted of twelve points: (1) the present time (1863) is the last dispensation; (2) Christ's Second Coming is imminent; (3) there will be no millennium of universal righteousness before Christ's Second Coming; (4) the church will not triumph before the Second Coming, but will remain cruciform; (5) Christ, not church institutions, is the only hope for the church; (6) Christ's Second Coming will initiate a new kind of justice based on heavenly rule rather than just destruction; (7) the saints, followed by those who lived a worthy life, will rise first to share in Christ's rule over a renewed world; (8) Christ will reign from Jerusalem, reflecting the glory of his transfiguration; (9) all existing institutions, be they church or state, will be judged in order to serve well in Christ's new world; (10) the Jews shall return to Palestine; (11) there will be a new heaven and a new earth, just as the old Adam is made new; and (12) only those who have been alert to the prophecies about the end time shall escape tribulation and share in Christ's glory. Although some of the points appear ambiguous, the editors of the *Prophetic Times* made it clear that millennialism is an essential part of both Christian hope and the American dream.

American millennial prophecy found its most popular expression in the famous *Scofield Reference Bible*. Cyrus Ingerson Scofield, a Tennessee lawyer who had Episcopal roots in Michigan, had been converted to Darbyite millennialism by James H. Brooks, a Presbyterian minister in St. Louis and a leader of the millennial–dispensationalist cause. After serving in Robert E. Lee's confederate army, Scofield turned to the ministry and to millennialism in 1882 when he became the pastor of the First Congregational Church in Dallas, Texas. He visited various Bible and prophecy conferences, propagating Darbyite dispensationalism. The center of Scofield's theological activities was the Correspondence Bible School, which became the Dallas Theological Seminary in 1924. He published his *Reference Bible* in 1909 and, with the aid of associates, amplified and amended it in 1919.[4]

Two concerns dominate Scofield's millennialism: to understand all of human history in terms of ages or dispensations which disclose the history of salvation, climaxing in the advent of the millennium, and to distinguish between Christians and Jews. Accordingly, there are seven dispensations: (1) the age of innocence, the covenant between God and Adam in Eden; (2) the age of conscience, the covenant between God and Adam after the Fall; (3) the age of human government, the covenant between God and Noah after the Flood; (4) the age of promise, the covenant between God and Abraham, in whom Israel is chosen; (5) the age of law, the covenant between God and Moses, ending with the crucifixion of Jesus by Jews and Gentiles; (6) the age of grace, the covenant in and through Jesus for individual Jews and Gentiles until the Second Coming of Christ; and (7) the age of the fulness of time, the millennium of Christ, and the restoration of the Davidian kingdom.

The *Scofield Reference Bible* presents the ancient scheme of salvation history in the cloak of Darbyite millennialism. Greek church fathers like Irenaeus and Latin church fathers like Augustine were concerned with the end time but did not devise a scheme of successive covenants or dispensations. Scofield's Bible, however, contains not only Old Testament promises and New Testament fulfillments but also the seven specific covenants which disclose God's plan for the world. Knowing God's plan and communicating its details were the most important concerns of millennial ministry during the time from the Civil War to World War I, seen as great tribulations of the end time.

A DRIVE FOR HOLINESS

If one wing of the Anglo-American millennialists disclosed a concern for the chronology of the end of the world, the other wing strove for "holiness" before the Second Coming of Christ. This holiness would be characterized by the gifts of the Holy Spirit such as visions, healings, and the drive to overcome the immorality of the world through "perfection."

Whereas dispensational millennialism dominated Presbyterianism, the holiness revival dominated American Methodism, the most successful religious movement in the nineteenth century. John Wesley had already expressed a strong concern for perfection, which he described as the culminating experience of the Christian life: it begins with "justification" by God through Christ, and it is nurtured in "sanctification" through the Holy Spirit. According to the *Plain Account of Christian Perfection* of 1777, incorporated into the Methodist *Discipline* of 1789, one year after Wesley's death, justified and sanctified persons go on to perfection, which is "purity of intention," "having the mind of Christ," and "the gradual work of circumcision of the heart from filthiness." Although Wesley insisted that sinless perfection can never be achieved because of the constant "residue of sin within," he saw perfection as the most powerful component of sanctification, the "second work of grace" (justification being the "first work"). Perfection, then, is a perfection of motives and desires, leading to "growth in grace." In this sense, perfection is "the grand deposition which God has lodged with the people called Methodist."[5]

Perfectionism, generally understood as a drive for holiness, had become the focus of a revival which climaxed after the end of the Civil War. In 1866, many Methodists celebrated the centenary of their beginnings in America by launching a crusade for holiness. In 1867, a "holiness camp meeting" in Vineland, New Jersey, spurred the creation of the National Camp Meeting Association for the Promotion of Holiness, which was supported by Methodist bishops and by such institutions of higher learning as Drew Seminary and Syracuse University. Many "holiness evangelists" appeared in Methodist and other churches, most of them not officially commissioned by bishops. Holiness literature, such as the popular periodical *Banner of Holiness*, flooded the cities of the North and the farms of the South; holiness preachers denounced the established Methodist church as a breeding ground for unsanctified worldliness; and a "come-outism" movement organized "holiness associations" in various parts of the country.

A clash between holiness dissidents and the Methodist bishops was inevitable. The General Conference of the Methodist Episcopal Church finally ousted the dissident holiness movement in 1894—a move which holiness evangelists regarded as a sure sign that Methodism had succumbed to worldliness and apostasy.

A number of independent holiness churches were founded between the 1890s and 1920s. Among the larger ones are the Pilgrim Holiness Church, which united several factions between 1897 and 1922, and the Church of the Nazarene, officially organized in 1908 at Pilot Point, Texas, when various associations merged for the sake of a common "pentecostal" witness.

One of the most radical movements was the Fire-Baptized Holiness Church, founded in 1895 by Benjamin Hardin Irwin, a native of Missouri and a Baptist preacher who had moved to Iowa. Influenced by the writings of John Fletcher (one of John Wesley's co-workers), he called for a "third experience" besides justification and sanctification—"the baptism with the Holy Ghost and fire" (or just "the fire") based on Acts 2:3, which speaks of "tongues of fire." Most holiness groups soon became familiar with Irwin's teachings, which he propagated at revival meetings and in his periodical *Live Coals of Fire*. But Irwin's influence diminished radically in 1900 when he confessed publicly that he had lived a life of "open and gross" sin leading to apostasy. The leadership of the Fire-Baptized Church was subsequently taken over by others, and the church lost its influence in the holiness movement.

Most of the holiness associations selected the name Church of

God and continued to stress millennial hope and holiness as the two basic strains of the gospel. Pentecostal prophecy and holiness revival had become institutionalized, though many members and leaders of holiness denominations shared the millennial dispensational pessimism regarding Christian institutions and expected the imminent return of Christ as the harbinger of a kingdom without earthly structures.

The unifying factor in the Anglo–American concern for the end time is what historians of American Christianity call "dispensational premillennialism," the conviction that there is an age of tribulation before the millennium of righteousness initiated at the Second Coming of Christ. As Sidney E. Ahlstrom says in *A Religious History of the American People:*

> Animating this new impulse [a concern for the end time] was a two-fold conviction that the whole Christian world, including the United States and Canada, was falling into apostasy and heresy so deeply and so decisively that it could only mean the approach of the Last Days; and that, therefore, nothing was more direly needed than the preaching of the hard facts drawn from God's Word. The body of doctrine on which these men gradually converged, however, was more than "the precious doctrine of Christ's second appearing." They searched out God's "whole pattern for the ages," and gradually a distinct system of dispensational premillennialism unified this intense "Bible study" movement and informed its conferences.[6]

Anglo–American millennialists considered the cataclysmic events of the American and French Revolutions as signs of the end time and as clues to the imminent return of Christ. The Civil War and World War I further nurtured millennial thought. Radical dispensational millennialists were convinced that events such as World War I would lead to the final battle between good and evil prophesied as "Armageddon" in Rev. 16:16. They perceived a number of clues pointing to the end of the world and the beginning of Christ's kingdom: the Reconstruction era after 1865; urbanization; the immigration of Europeans; natural science with its agnostic tendencies; disrespect for biblical authority, especially among literary critics; the invasion of the theory of evolution into public education; religious apathy in the mainline denominations; the lack of a Protestant consensus in the face of a growing Roman Catholic and Jewish population; the waning of belief in patriotism based on America's role as moral leader of the world; and the religious, cultural, and political pluralism which threatened what was assumed to be a divinely instituted synthesis of the American dream and evangelical Christianity.

PITFALLS

Historical research has revealed that there is a close link between millennialist proclamations and revolutionary ideology, especially in times of crisis. Those who prophesy about the end of the world usually form revolutionary cadres opposed to the existing status quo, which they see as the final stage before the beginning of a new and better Christ-ruled world. Luther's reform movement, for example, attracted Thomas Müntzer and the "Zwickau prophets" (from the Saxon town of Zwickau), who regarded the Peasants War and the invasion of the Turks in the 1520s as clues to the imminent end of the world. As a consequence, Müntzer and the Zwickau prophets called for the abolition of the organized church and of the state to make way for the free rule of the Holy Spirit, who would lead people to proper repentance. These prophets (Luther labeled them *Schwärmer*, that is, "swarming spirits") claimed to have had charismatic experiences, either through visions or through other "fruits of the Holy Spirit," which gave them special insights into the divine plan of history.

Though Luther also expected the imminent end of the world, he opposed charismatic speculations about the end time, considering them to be diabolic distortions of the way in which God discloses divine caring and redeeming love for humankind. In an extensive treatise on the subject of charismatic prophecy, Luther reminded his followers that God reveals the "good news," the gospel, first outwardly and only then inwardly: outwardly through audible and visible forms of communication such as speaking, hearing, baptismal washing, and eucharistic eating and drinking; inwardly through the Holy Spirit and spiritual gifts, especially the gift of faithful trust. "God has determined to give the inward to no one except through the outward," Luther contended, citing ample biblical evidence to prove his point. Tampering with this revealed order is the work of the devil, the "confuser" (*diabolos*). "With all

25

his mouthing of the words, 'Spirit, Spirit, Spirit,' he tears down the bridge, the path, the way, the ladder, and all means by which the Spirit might come to you."[7]

Norman Cohn has argued that the pursuit of the millennium in Western Christendom, especially during the Middle Ages and the Reformation, created part of the ideological foundation for the modern tyrannies embodied in Nazism and Communism:

> As in the Nazi apocalypse the "Aryan race" was to purify the earth by annihilating the "Jewish race," so in the Communist apocalypse the "bourgeoisie" is to be exterminated by the "proletariat." And here too we are faced with a secularized version of a phantasy that is many centuries old . . . . A boundless, millennial promise made with boundless, prophet-like conviction to a number of rootless and desperate men in the midst of a society where traditional norms and relationships are disintegrating—here, it would seem, lay the source of that peculiar subterranean fanaticism which subsisted as a perpetual menace to the structure of medieval society. It may be suggested that here, too, lies the source of the giant fanaticisms which in our day have convulsed the world.[8]

Apocalyptic gospel communication tends to sidestep and perhaps even forget altogether the central Christian testimony that Christ calls believers into service in *this* world, not into a position of waiting for the world to come. Christian teaching about the end time (eschatology, from *eschaton*, the last) does not call us to speculate about the end time, but to be alert to the "signs of the times" which provide clues to what needs to be done now in this world. "Take heed, watch; for you do not know when the time will come" (Mark 13:33). Watching for the return of Christ should not paralyze believers; instead, they should be encouraged to continue their witness in word and deed as they await Christ's return despite their failures and shortcomings.

Christian hope becomes lame when it is reduced to the consolation that "things will get better" in the next world. Instead, Christian hope should be the realistic foundation for concrete ethical action, and as such, should avoid Utopian idealism.

The gospel calls for a cruciform life on earth, that is, a life fully aware of sin, evil, and death, yet committed to the living Lord who will come at the end of time. To be oriented exclusively toward the end time can be the signal that Christian hope has been paralyzed by the fear that faith is without influence in the world. Apocalyptic gospel communication discloses the perennial Christian anxiety about the success of the witness to the resurrected Lord. This anxiety has created both Utopian activists, who want to make the world ready for Christ, and groups of God's "frozen people," who consider their time and place to be the divine kingdom and thus refuse to deal with the world.

NOTES

1. For an elaboration of this difference, see Charles N. Cochrane, *Christianity and Classical Culture: Thought and Action from Augustus to Augustine* (New York: Oxford University Press, 1957), especially chap. 11.

2. For a history of millennialism and its contemporary significance, see Norman Cohn, *The Pursuit of the Millennium: Revolutionary Messianism in Medieval and Reformation Europe and Its Bearing on Modern Totalitarian Movements*, 2d ed. (New York: Harper Torch Books, 1961). On Joachim of Floris, see chap. 5.

3. Quoted in Ernest R. Sandeen, *The Roots of Fundamentalism: British and American Millenarianism, 1800-1930* (Chicago: University of Chicago Press, 1970), p. 44. This is a seminal study which demonstrates that American fundamentalism is rooted in millennialism. The author summarizes the findings of this rather substantial book in a pamphlet entitled *Toward an Historical Understanding of the Origins of Fundamentalism*, ed. Richard C. Wolf, Facet Books Historical Series (Philadelphia: Fortress Press, 1968).

4. The first edition was issued in 1909 by Oxford University Press in New York. A 1966 edition, revised by several dispensationalists, has become one of the most popular religious books in recent times.

5. Quoted in Sidney E. Ahlstrom, *A Religious History of the American People* (New Haven: Yale University Press, 1972), p. 816, n. 8. This is the most comprehensive study of religion in America and a very useful reference work.

6. Ibid., p. 808. The context of this quotation is a discussion of "Dissent and Reaction in Protestantism" between the Civil War and World War I.

7. "Against the Heavenly Prophets," in *Luther's Works*, American Edition, vol. 40 (Philadelphia: Fortress Press, 1958), pp. 146–47.

8. Cohn, *Pursuit of the Millennium*, pp. 311 and 319.

2

The Fundamentalist Movement

HEAD RELIGION

A drive for intellectual certainty has always been present in Christian history, especially in the West. This drive has been decisively influenced by the Greek metaphysical tradition associated with Plato and Aristotle. According to this tradition, reality consists of "essences" or "substances" which have "attributes" or "accidents." The state of being a human being, for example, is "substance," and that of being rational is "attribute." Substances and attributes are the necessary ingredients for any logical argument: all human beings are rational; Caesar is a human being; therefore Caesar is rational. These three statements together constitute a "syllogism." One must recognize, however, that there are two kinds of substance: "material" and "spiritual." Material substances are temporal and divisible and fall short of the ideal of being self-subsistent with their attributes; they are perceived by the senses and known through physics (from *physis*, meaning "nature"). Spiritual substances are timeless and indivisible and remain quite self-subsistent; they cannot be perceived by the senses and are known through metaphysics (from *meta physis*, meaning "that which is beyond nature").

All of reality is perceived by this distinction. How do human beings know spiritual substances? Although there are various answers to this question, an argument of abstraction prevails: either material reality is abstracted from spiritual reality (Plato's argument is that true reality is spiritual and hidden, and what the senses perceive are shadows of this reality), or vice versa (Aristotle's assumption is that the many substances must have one source, a "prime mover," who is timeless and immortal). Human beings share timeless immortality with the prime mover through their immortal soul.

There is, then, a pyramidlike hierarchical order of reality consisting of material (natural) and spiritual (supernatural) substances whose relationships with each other can be perceived in various ways by the human mind, which glimpses eternal truth through the immortal soul—the one substance which, according to Aristotle, connects physical and metaphysical realities like an umbilical cord. Thus the meaning of reality accords to the classification of all substances on the basis of a logical order of being (ontology) disclosed by the one and only source of the universe, the prime mover, God.

Medieval scholastic theology used the Greek metaphysical vision of reality to justify the medieval fusion of Christianity and culture and to compete with Islamic religion. Theologians were dedicated to the principle "I believe in order to understand," the motto of Anselm of Canterbury (1033–1109). A number of theological issues could be settled by using these ontological distinctions of reality, as the system of Thomas Aquinas (1255–1274) discloses. For example, it is quite helpful to argue, as the sixteenth-century Protestant Aristotelians did, that there is a difference between the confession "We are *by nature* sinful and unclean" and the confession "We are *in substance* sinful and unclean." For the substance of human beings is both to be and to remain creatures of God, even though "by nature" (in their attributes or accidents) they are transgressors who have inherited the sin of Adam and Eve. Human beings, therefore, still remain "created in the image of God"; they are made sinners not by God but by the Fall. When simple-minded Christians become confused by the seemingly contradictory biblical assertions of a "good creation" and "original sin," clever theological minds comfort them with the argument that logical necessity demands a distinction between the *substance* of creation and the *accident* of sin. Hence, an evil humankind, having inherited the sin of Adam and Eve, nevertheless lives in God's creation, which is *substantially* good.

Greek metaphysical language and modes of thought have occasionally invaded the Protestant tradition, even though the early Protestant reformers considered the medieval combination of Athens and Jerusalem a distortion of the gospel of God incarnate in Jesus of Israel. In the seventeenth century, for example, a German movement called *Orthodoxy* (meaning "correct teaching") applied the Aristotelian mode of thought to Luther's theology in order to create a coherent system of Christian ideas and morality. Subsequently, "the importance of a particular doctrine came to depend on its place in the system rather than upon its practical relation to life."[1] German universities, including the University of Wittenberg, contributed to this revival of Aristotle's thought in an effort to create uniform doctrine and life in Lutheran territories. In 1577, doctrinal controversies were settled by a "formula of concord" which used Greek metaphysical language and patterns of thought to defend Luther and the truth of the gospel.[2] Systematic attempts to communicate the gospel in this way culminated in elaborate systematic theologies and codes of ethics. John Gerhard, a Lutheran, presented his *Loci theologici* in 1610, which illustrate the shift from Luther's fundamental concern for oral gospel communication to an extremely cognitive, doctrinal elaboration of the gospel, leading to a system of logical thought and moral action. According to Gerhard, theology involves a double conception: (1) a systematic and abstract "teaching drawn from the Word of God by which men are instructed in true faith and true piety to eternal life"; and (2) a concrete "divinely given habit conferred on man by the Holy Spirit through the Word." In this manner, "men, imbued with true faith and good works, are led to the kingdom of heaven."[3]

> Theology accordingly has a double function. The formal and objective criterion entails that theological statements can be seen by any intelligent person (who is not prevented "by age or ignorance") to be drawn from Scripture. The dialectical and personal criterion entails that a theological statement is effective in concrete proclamation—when spoken by a person with the divinely given *habitus* it has the power to be heard as the *vox Dei*. The two are interdependent. Nothing can really be concretely effective if it is not objectively true; and everything which is objectively true (that is, drawn from Scripture) has the latent power of being concretely effective.[4]

John Gerhard and other Protestant scholastic theologians worked with the philosophical presupposition, later employed by nineteenth-century fundamentalists, that there is a connection between the reality of faith and the reality of reason. They understood this connection as "ontological," according to the distinction between "physical" and "metaphysical" reality in the Greek metaphysical tradition. Theology was to show that what is believed is objectively true, and that what is objectively true can be believed. Scripture must therefore be objectively true because it is inspired by God; consequently, Scripture is to be believed and, when it is believed, human lives will change. In this sense "theoretical" theology leads to "practical" piety.

Whereas medieval scholastic theologians used the ontological distinctions to settle doctrinal controversies, philosophers of the eighteenth-century Enlightenment used them to inquire into the mystery of nature and human inter-relationships. Voltaire in France, Wilhelm Leibnitz in Germany, and David Hume in England regarded the Judeo-Christian God as the prime mover of a world governed by an intricate system of laws that human reason would understand and that could be used to create a better world. The German thinker Immanuel Kant (1724–1804) and his English disciple David Hume (1711–1776) taught that "facts" are "phenomena," recognized and understood only through the imposition of categories furnished by the interpreting human mind. The difference between "real" facts (a priori facts, such as God and immortality) and "historical" facts is established through critical interpretations which take into account the category of time.

Deism, a philosophical movement which originated in England at the time of the Enlightenment, assumed that God is indifferent to and powerless in the created world. Only God's highest creatures, human beings, can bring about change and progress by using pragmatic rational principles based on an understanding of "natural laws." Deism underlay the political philosophy of the founders of the United States, especially Thomas Jefferson, one of the most influential of the "religious rationalists."[5] The one dollar bill, on which the creed "In God We Trust" is flanked by the Great Seal of the United States, clearly symbolizes deism's influence on political philosophy. One side of the seal depicts an Egyptian pyramid topped by the eye of God, a popular Free Mason symbol. It carries an inscription adapted from the chief work of the Roman poet Virgil (70–19 B.C.), who announced that the "golden age" had begun in 40 B.C. with the reign of Caesar Augustus Octavian (*Eclogae* IV.5): "The year of the new order of centuries" (*annuit coeptis, novus ordo seculorum*), and the year is 1776. The other side of the seal bears the slogan "one out of many" (*e pluribus unum*), a description of the democratic foundation of the nation; thirteen stars for the original thirteen states; and a watchful eagle carrying the symbols of war and peace.

PRINCETON THEOLOGY AND
NIAGARA PROPHECY

The pragmatic rationalists, deists, and scientists who, under the influence of the eighteenth-century Enlightenment, laid the foundation for revolutions in politics, culture, and the understanding of life in general, were bound to clash with millennialists. They no longer regarded the Bible as a reliable source of knowledge concerning the beginning or the end of life. Their "evidence" contradicted that of biblical cosmology and anthropology. Moreover, the application of rationalistic, scientific methods to biblical studies threatened cherished notions about God, Jesus, and the world. When radical liberals such as David F. Strauss declared in his *Life of Jesus* (1835) that the divinity of Jesus was a "myth," orthodox defenders of biblical truth organized a spirited defense against the onslaught of modernist thought.

Millennial Bible study institutes such as the Nyack Missionary College in New York, the Moody Bible Institute in Chicago, and the Bible Institute of Los Angeles, provided training for evangelical missionaries. But it was the Presbyterian seminary in Princeton, New Jersey, that became the bulwark of the biblical strand of millennialism and theological apologetics (later known as fundamentalism) against modernist biblical criticism and agnostic rationalism. Founded in 1812, the seminary had been known for its staunch defense of reformed Calvinist doctrine against Unitarian and other liberal trends in theology. Its first professor, Archibald Alexander, supported the view that Christianity is based on "evidence" which can withstand the test of scientific method. Charles Hodge was Alexander's most famous student and also his successor. Hodge edited the *Biblical Repertory and Princeton Review* for more than forty years and summarized his work in a three-volume *Systematic Theology* (1872–73).

The focus of "Princeton theology" was on the authority of inspired Scripture. Grounded in the Greek metaphysical tradition, it assumed that God was supernatural and perfect, whereas human beings were not. Whenever God became involved in something, such as the creation of holy Scripture, then it too had to be perfect or, at least, basically without fault. The Bible was therefore perceived as participating in the supernatural and perfect qualities of God and, consequently, as containing truth without error and the promise of salvation from an imperfect world.

Hodge's argument was quite clear: natural science and theology were two equally significant scholarly enterprises. Natural science arranges and systematizes the facts of the general world to ascertain the laws by which they are determined; theology systematizes the facts of the Bible in order to ascertain the principles or general truths which those facts involve. The scientific foundation of biblical truth was the infallibility and divine authority of the Scriptures,

> due to the fact that they are the word of God; and they are the word of God because they were given by the inspiration of the Holy Ghost . . . . If the sacred writers assert that they are the organs of God . . . then, if we believe their divine mission, we must believe what they teach as to the nature of the influence under which they spoke and wrote.[6]

In 1881, Hodge and Benjamin B. Warfield, who had joined the Princeton faculty in the defense of Calvinist doctrine and biblical inerrancy, clinched their arguments in favor of biblical literalism with a doctrine of biblical inerrancy: God put the actual words into the mouths of the biblical writers (Jer. 1:9); their words can be proven to be consistent with known facts in history and science, though never perfectly; some errors of detail do not, however, demonstrate the errancy of all of Scripture; on the whole, biblical texts are the original autographs of the Holy Spirit through the pens of the authors who faithfully recorded what the Holy Spirit dictated.[7]

Hodge and Warfield used these arguments to interpret the *Westminster Confession* of 1646, which taught that the "infallible truth and divine authority" of the word of God "is from the inward work of the Holy Spirit, bearing witness by and with the Word in our hearts." This definition is rooted in Calvin's notion of the internal testimony of the Holy Spirit.[8] These Princeton theologians wanted to show that it is reasonable to hold the doctrine that the unity and meaning of Scripture—the container of the infallible word of God—are inspired, even though some words in their grammatical structure may not be.

Underlying the Princeton theology was the conviction that reason and revelation do not diverge, as most mystics and rationalists argue, but rather converge. Whereas philosophical reason works by speculation, induction, and syllogism, theological reason ascertains the biblical facts of divine authority and demonstrates how they are in harmony with philosophical and scientific facts. Whenever the revealed facts of the Bible disagree with the facts of philosophy and science, the latter must yield to the former, for there cannot be a *real* contradiction between reason and revelation. Since, for example, Scripture reveals that Jesus was the Son of God, all other evidence concerning Jesus (when he lived, what he said, what situations influenced him) is to be subordinated to the revealed truth that he was the Son of God who came to save humankind from sin.

Princeton theology assumed certain fundamentals, based on the divinity of Jesus as the indispensable *fundamentum* of all truth and salvation, and then looked for evidence of these fundamentals in the Bible, the primary source of this truth. While such theology represents circular argumentation (the premise determines the argument, and the argument proves the truth of the premise), it comforts those who are already "fundamentalists," that is, those who share its basic assumptions. They are provided with a "theologic" which establishes the desired harmony between faith and reason. Those who do not share a belief in the same fundamentals, however, remain unconvinced. That is why fundamentalists had such a hard time convincing nonfundamentalists of their truths.

To present a united front against liberals and modernists within and outside the Presbyterian church, general assemblies in the 1880s affirmed the Princeton theology. Scholars who applied the historical–critical method to biblical studies and to Calvinist doctrine were dismissed for heresy or resigned from the ministry. Two Old Testament scholars, C. A. Briggs at Union Seminary in New York and Henry P. Smith at Lane Seminary in Cincinnati, were dismissed from their posts in 1893. A. C. McGiffert, famous historian of New Testament literature and the early church at Union Seminary, resigned from the ministry in 1900. The 1892 general assembly adopted the Hodge–Warfield doctrine of biblical inerrancy in its Portland Deliverance, which held that the "inspired Word, as it comes from God [in the original autographs] is without error." The 1910 general assembly declared the doctrine of biblical inerrancy "essential and necessary," making it the cornerstone of the Five Points which have become the creed of fundamentalists: (1) the Bible is inspired and without error; (2) Jesus was born of a virgin; (3) his death atoned for the sins of all people ("satisfaction theory" or "substitutionary atonement"); (4) there will be a resurrection "with the same body"; and (5) the miracles of Jesus are real and true.[9]

Classical fundamentalists generally have argued the position that the Bible is authoritative because it is inspired and therefore inerrant. How do we know? According to most fundamentalist polemicists, we know because the Bible says so; Jesus, Paul, Peter, and other speakers in the Bible make the same claim. Since they know what God has revealed, they are trustworthy sources. More important, since the Bible contains the revelation that Jesus was the Son of God, whatever Jesus said and whatever has been said about him by those who knew him, must be true. As one fundamentalist put it, "If the evangelists were guilty of trifling errors and evidences of carelessness in so-called minor matters, we simply cannot escape the conclusion that they may have been just as careless in more important things."[10] Arguments like these use biblical and theological assertions (for example, that Jesus was the Son of God) to establish the historical inerrancy of the Bible (for example, that Jonah was, indeed, factually in the belly of a big fish since Jesus compared his work of redemption to Jonah's three days and nights in the belly of the fish, Matt. 12:40).

Although these general assemblies did not set forth millennial speculations, subsequent Bible and prophecy conferences clearly demonstrated the alliance between the Princeton theology and millennial prophecy.

In 1868, founders of the millennial periodical, *Waymarks in the Wilderness*, convened the first conference of Bible study and millennial prophecy in New York City. George H. Bishop, a graduate of

Princeton, and George C. Needham, an immigrant preacher from Ireland, planned and led this conference and other similar ones in St. Louis, Philadelphia, and Galt, Ontario. After 1875, additional conferences were held in Chicago for several years. Then, from 1883 until 1897, the conferences, lasting one or two weeks, took place usually during the summer at Niagara-on-the-Lake, Ontario, and came to be called the Niagara Conference. Eventually, one hundred and twenty leaders directed the Niagara Conference, which was dominated by the Darbyite Presbyterian pastor James Hall Brookes. Brookes was also one of the major contributors to the periodical *Waymarks in the Wilderness*.

Darbyite methods of biblical interpretation prevailed at the Niagara Conference; the rapture of the church from the earth and the secret Second Coming of Christ were favorite topics of discussion. The 1884 conference even developed the custom of ringing bells at dawn and at other times of the day to symbolize the possibility of Christ's secret coming in accordance with what Darby had taught in his doctrine on the rapture.

The 1878 Niagara Creed, so called because its authors were later associated with the Niagara Conference, became the platform for a widespread Bible and prophecy movement. Its fourteen points stressed the verbal inspiration of the Bible and the premillennial coming of Christ: (1) the entire Bible is inspired by the Holy Spirit "to the smallest word and inflection of a word, provided such word is found in the original manuscripts"; (2) there is one God in three persons, all of whom share "the same nature, attributes and perfections" and are "worthy of precisely the same homage, confidence and obedience"; (3) the human creature is sinful after the Fall, having "totally lost all spiritual life"; (4) the sin of Adam and Eve is inherited, and human nature is "essentially and unchangeably bad ... incapable by any educational process whatever of subjecting itself to His [God's] law"; (5) "no one can enter the kingdom of God unless born again ... a new life implanted by the Holy Ghost through the Word is absolutely essential to salvation"; (6) salvation comes solely through Jesus Christ, not through anything or anyone else—be it penitence, faith, or "submission to the rules and regulations of any church"; (7) salvation is mediated "by faith alone," and "the moment we trust in Him [Christ] as our Saviour we pass out

37

of death into everlasting life"; (8) those who are born again are "assured of their salvation from the very day they take Him to be their Saviour," as Scripture testifies; (9) all of Scripture is about Christ, and "no chapter of even the Old Testament is properly read or understood until it leads to Him"; (10) the church consists of all who "are united by the Holy Spirit to the risen and ascended Son of God . . . rising above all sectarian prejudices and denominational bigotry"; (11) the Holy Spirit, "not as an influence, but as a Divine Person sustains the church and all believers . . . [and] is ever present to testify of Christ"; (12) everyone is called to a "holy calling or walk" after the Spirit, not the flesh, which needs to be subjected to Christ; (13) the immortal soul joins Christ immediately after death "until the resurrection of the body at His coming, when soul and body [are] reunited" while the souls of unbelievers "remain after death in conscious misery until the final judgment . . . at the close of the millennium, when soul and body reunited shall be cast into the lake of fire"; (14) the present age is marked by apostasy, and "the Lord Jesus will come in person to introduce the millennial age, when Israel shall be restored to their own land, and the earth shall be full of the knowledge of the Lord."[11]

Since the Niagara Conference did not satisfy many Darbyite millennialists, they convened the First American Bible and Prophetic Conference in 1878 at New York's Holy Trinity Episcopal Church. The economic depression that led to the panic of 1873, the contested election of 1876, and the railroad strike of 1877 precipitated still other conferences in 1886 and 1895. An emphasis on biblical inerrancy and dispensational millennialism prevailed at these conferences. Participants manifested hostility toward any "liberal" movement, be it historical–critical Bible study or any preaching about the end that denied the Second Coming of Christ either after a time of trial and tribulation or without warning. The most influential revivalist of the nineteenth century, Dwight L. Moody, invited many speakers of the Niagara Conference and of the Bible and Prophetic Conferences to his own conferences, which were held in Northfield, Massachusetts, from 1880 until his death in 1899. Bible institutes and Sunday schools became the chief instruments of dissemination of the fundamentals.

THE FUNDAMENTALS

The drive to unite Anglo–American Protestants through agreement on fundamental truths reached its peak with the publication of *The Fundamentals* between 1910 and 1915. Published with the "compliments of two Christian laymen," the periodicals had eleven editions. Three million copies were sent free of charge to "English-speaking Protestant pastors, evangelists, missionaries, theological students, Y.M.C.A. secretaries, Y.W.C.A. secretaries, Sunday school superintendents, religious lay workers, and editors of religious publications throughout the earth."

The two laymen were brothers, Lyman and Milton Stewart, natives of Pennsylvania, who had made a fortune in oil. Both were chief stockholders in the Union Oil Company in Los Angeles and Chicago, and Lyman was company president. A member of Immanuel Presbyterian Church in Los Angeles, Lyman became a Darbyite millennialist, supporting causes that alerted the world to Christ's Second Coming and propagated biblical literalism and millennialism. Both Lyman and Milton Stewart lamented the growing laxity in matters of faith and morals among Presbyterians. Milton turned his attention to the missionary enterprise, especially in China; Lyman supported educational institutions committed to Bible study, such as Occidental College and the Bible Institute in Los Angeles. Finally, Lyman became the enthusiastic supporter of a plan to commit the English-speaking Protestant world to a unique effort of evangelization by the publication of *The Fundamentals*. The idea for the enterprise appears to have originated with Amzi Clarence Dixon, the millennialist preacher at the Moody Church in Chicago.

Lyman met Dixon in 1909 and gave him $300,000 toward the gigantic literary undertaking. Milton Stewart also gave his financial backing to the venture. Dixon then established an editorial committee consisting of three clergy and three lay members, all of whom had millennial leanings. Sixty-four authors were chosen to write articles for the periodical, most of them British and American millennialist veterans. Of the ninety articles that appeared, twenty-nine defended biblical literalism, thirty-one argued the fundamental doctrines of the Princeton theology and the Five Points of the 1910 General Presbyterian Assembly, and the rest were personal testimonies, attacks on science, and proposals for mission.

The movement called "fundamentalist" found its literary basis in *The Fundamentals.*[12] Lyman Stewart's Testimony Publishing Company received two hundred thousand letters praising the movement he had helped to launch. Presbyterian, Methodist, Baptist, and Lutheran church leaders regarded *The Fundamentals* as a serious scholarly enterprise aimed at Christian unity. The *Theological Quarterly* of The Lutheran Church–Missouri Synod, for example, called the fundamentalist series "the most grateful surprise which this year's [1911] book market has brought us," although Lutheran theories concerning the fundamental notion of biblical inspiration have roots in seventeenth-century Lutheran orthodoxy rather than in twentieth-century fundamentalism.[13] Fundamentalists supported the *Scofield Reference Bible,* became linked with the American Bible League which was founded in 1903, and taught a premillennial dispensationalism.

The inspiration of the Bible and speculations about Christ's Second Coming dominated the movement before World War I. Biblical literalism, which had been the steady companion of millennial hopes, was the center of fundamentalism. The five articles in *The Fundamentals* on the inspiration of the Bible are based on the Princeton theology of Warfield and Hodge. One of the authors, James M. Gray, dean of the Moody Bible Institute in Chicago, clearly reflected fundamentalist concerns for biblical authority and prophecy:

> The character of its [the Bible's] contents, the unity of its parts, the fulfillment of its prophecies, the miracles wrought in its attestation, the effects it has accomplished in the lives of nations and of men, all these go to show that it is divine, and if so, that it may be believed in what it says about itself.[14]

Whereas *The Fundamentals* did not succeed in uniting conservative English-speaking Protestants around the world, they did supply the ammunition needed to defend fundamental Christian truths against modernist errors. The main targets of the fundamentalist crusade were biblical "higher criticism," which distinguished between spiritual and scientific truths in the Bible (for example, higher criticism claims that the Bible discloses salvation in Christ but not the geological age of the world); Charles Darwin's theory of evolution, which argued the descent of humans from an anthropoid animal (*The Descent of Man*, 1871); and the theology of a "social gospel," which envisaged the kingdom of God not as a future millennium, but as a socioeconomic struggle between those who share their profit with the poor in the name of Jesus and those who do not (the argument of the Baptist theologian Walter Rauschenbusch in *A Theology for the Social Gospel*, 1917). In its defense of biblical literalism and millennialism, *The Fundamentals* launched a movement of conservative scholars and church leaders who feared the collapse of what they thought to be a "Protestant consensus" in America. They argued that such a collapse was essentially precipitated by the majority of mainline denominations which, attempting to be "in the world," fell prey to the satanic forces of modernism. Bible institutes, prophecy conferences, and the Sunday school movement disseminated the findings of *The Fundamentals*, thus providing fundamentalism with a broad base of operation.

CONFLICTS AND CONFLUENCES

Millennialists and biblical literalists agreed that World War I was a God-sent event to urge the world to do penance for its sins. British and American prophecy conferences revived millennial hopes for the imminent Second Coming of Christ. A Philadelphia conference in May 1918 and a New York conference which celebrated the end of the war in November 1918 focused on the classic Darbyite themes of the gathering of the Jews in Jerusalem (which city, incidentally, had been conquered by the British) and the coming of the Lord after the tribulation of World War I. Bible institutes, led by the Moody Bible Institute of Chicago, trained thousands of people to become defenders of biblical inerrancy and prevailing millennialist views. In 1919, a cadre of prophecy conference leaders founded the World's Christian Fundamentals Association in Philadelphia to provide a corporate structure for fundamentalism separate from other denominational and interdenominational organizations such as the Federal Council of Churches.

Affirming the basic stance of *The Fundamentals*, the Association held a World's Conference on Christian Fundamentals in the summer of 1919 in Philadelphia, which resulted in the creation of five permanent committees to defend the fundamentals of Christianity against the modernist errors of the mainline denominations. These committees were charged with (1) accrediting Bible schools on the basis of subscription to the doctrine of biblical inspiration and other fundamentals resembling the Five Points of the 1910 Presbyterian General Assembly; (2) attacking modernism, especially through educational institutions; (3) using religious periodicals to disseminate fundamentalist views; (4) organizing Bible conferences to reach as many Americans as possible; and (5) strengthening and expanding existing fundamentalist foreign missionary societies, especially in China and Africa. The stage was set for an encounter between the Protestant denominational establishment and the fundamentalist dissenters.

It was the famous Baptist preacher Harry E. Fosdick who challenged the fundamentalist cause in 1922 with a sermon published in the *Christian Century* entitled "Shall Fundamentalists Win?" While a missionary in China, Fosdick had become increasingly concerned about the biblical literalism and speculative millennialism propagated by American missionaries. He used his influence as a teacher at Union Theological Seminary and as a regular guest preacher at the First Presbyterian Church in New York to say no to fundamentalism because of its exclusivist and legalistic stance.

When the conflict began to affect the rank and file of the Presbyterian church, the general assemblies of 1923 and 1924 voted to bring the First Presbyterian Church of New York in line with the Five Points and to invite Fosdick to join the Presbyterian clergy since his preaching, as a Baptist among Presbyterians, was an "anomalous situation." Fosdick resigned from the First Presbyterian Church because he could not accept the doctrinal assertions of the Five Points. After a brief pastorate at the Park Avenue Baptist Church, he became interdenominational minister at Riverside Church in New York, which had been built in 1931 through the generosity of John D. Rockefeller.

But the conflict started by Fosdick continued. In 1924, twelve hundred Presbyterians submitted the Auburn Affirmation to the general assembly, protesting a fundamentalist stance and calling for the preservation of the unity and freedom of the church. Nevertheless, a schism urged by church conservatives and led by the Princeton professor of New Testament, J. Gresham Machen, seemed imminent. Machen had called for a clear separation of modern liberalism from fundamental Christianity in his book *Christianity and Liberalism*—the "Bible" of American fundamentalism since its publication in 1923. The Presbyterian general assemblies of 1925, 1926, and 1927, however, refused to yield to fundamentalist pressure, arguing that the Presbyterian system permits different points of view and that local presbyteries had the authority to license and ordain ministers even though they might not always conform to all the decisions of the general assemblies.

By 1929, Princeton Seminary rather than the Presbyterian church experienced the schism which fundamentalists had urged: the Machen disciples seceded from Princeton to organize their own Westminster Seminary in Philadelphia. In addition, the separatists from Princeton and the Scofield millennialists united to form the Presbyterian Church of America after they lost the battle for control of the foreign mission in the Presbyterian church. However, disagreements between moderate and radical factions in the new Presbyterian Church of America precipitated a walkout of those who adhered to a Scofield-type millennialism. These millennialists were led by Carl McIntyre (a 1929 graduate of Princeton) and other radicals who founded the Bible Presbyterian Synod in 1937. This synod claimed to adhere to the Westminster Confession of 1646, except "in any particular in which the premillennial teaching of the Scriptures may be held to be obscured."[15] Once again, the confluence of biblical and millennial fundamentalists had led to conflict between moderate and radical theological views. Whereas many Presbyterian fundamentalists were absorbed by the mainline denomination, the Bible Presbyterian Synod became the base for the antiecumenical and anticommunist crusades of Carl McIntyre and his disciples in the 1940s and 1950s.

Not only Presbyterians but Baptists too became embroiled in fundamentalist conflicts. Baptist fundamentalists created the Conferences on Fundamentals of Our Baptist Faith in 1920 to express their opposition to liberal theology and natural science. "Counterseminaries," such as the Northern Baptist Seminary in Chicago

(1913) and Eastern Seminary in Philadelphia (1925), were founded to curb the influence of such liberal schools as Chicago Divinity School and the Philadelphia Crozer Seminary. Annual conventions were the scenes of stormy debates, especially over the doctrine of biblical inerrancy. Amzi C. Dixon, editor of *The Fundamentals*, led a cadre of Northern Baptists against the modernist forces in the convention. The Dixon conservatives argued for agreement on doctrine (especially on the doctrine of biblical authority), a uniform approach to foreign mission based on doctrinal agreement, and the removal of liberal and modernist views from the seminaries. A majority of Northern Baptist clergy and laity in the late 1920s seemed to agree with these fundamentalist endeavors, but by the beginning of the 1930s schisms began to appear just as they had among Presbyterians. Fundamentalist Bible Institutes, Charles E. Fuller's "Old Fashioned Revival Hour" broadcast from Los Angeles, and independent congregations provided the impetus for secession from the mainline Northern Baptist denomination. In 1932, the General Association of Regular Baptists was organized, consisting of five hundred churches by 1946; in 1947, the Conservative Baptist Association was formed—a radical fundamentalist group with seminaries, a missionary society, and a quarter of a million members by 1969.

The Disciples of Christ also experienced conflict with fundamentalists. The focus of the fundamentalists' attack was Herbert L. Willett, professor of New Testament at the Chicago Divinity School, who led students and clergy in attempts to introduce modern critical biblical scholarship and theology into Sunday school as a means of fostering an ecumenical spirit. By 1927, some conservatives seceded and established the North American Christian Convention, later known as the Churches of Christ. Still, the mainline denomination was able to survive with both a liberal and a conservative wing and without a schism.

The most notorious aspect of American fundamentalism was its crusade against Darwin's theory of evolution.[16] Fundamentalist organizations, led by the World's Christian Fundamentals Association, initiated legislative efforts to curb the teaching of evolution in public schools, especially in the South. The most influential of these fundamentalist organizations was the Bible Crusaders of America, founded in 1925 with the financial assistance of George F.

Washburn, a wealthy Florida businessman who donated $200,000 to the Crusaders. The governor of Florida and several state senators became officers in the organization, which publicized its views in the *Crusaders' Champion*, a thirty-two page magazine eventually known for its slogan, "Back to Christ, the Bible, and the Constitution." Widely disseminated and read, the magazine embodied the fusion of fundamentalism and politics for the sake of saving America from the evils of modernism and evolution.

Three "remedies" were suggested by the *Champion* to cure the country of unchristian diseases: (1) the boycott of religious publications, missions, and educational institutions supporting modernism and evolution; (2) the organization of fundamentalists within the churches in order to expel liberals and elect conservatives to government; and (3) a drive for legislative action against unchristian science, especially evolution. Washburn himself proposed a constitutional amendment to make America Christian again. To begin his campaign, he offered to finance public debates between prominent fundamentalists and the famous trial lawyer Clarence Darrow "or any other agnostic, modernist, evolutionist, or atheist of equal prominence."

From 1925 to 1926, the Crusaders staged demonstrations and attempted to influence legislation in favor of antievolution laws in Florida, Tennessee, Mississippi, Louisiana, and North Carolina, but with no visible success. The Crusaders' blatant politics, their flaunting of large sums of money, and the attention focused on the Scopes trial in Dayton, Tennessee, seemed to drive more people away from the organization than to it. By the fall of 1926, the *Crusaders' Champion* had ceased publication and Washburn joined the cadre of itinerant fundamentalists speaking at national and international conventions.

The state of Tennessee in 1925 was not the first to pass a law against the teaching of evolution. Oklahoma had already done so two years before. But it was in Tennessee that such legislation was publicly tested. A biology teacher and athletic instructor at Dayton's Central High School, John T. Scopes, was found guilty of violating the state's antievolution law in the spring of 1925 and fined $100. The celebrated "monkey trial" in Dayton in July 1925 occurred when the American Civil Liberties Union requested that the constitutionality of Tennessee's antievolution law be tested in relation to the Scopes matter.

Over one hundred reporters attended the trial, which climaxed in the confrontation between the liberal Clarence Darrow and the fundamentalist crusader William J. Bryan (the latter had been the losing presidential candidate against William McKinley in 1896). Fundamentalist sentiment dominated throughout Dayton, where southern conservatives wanted to take a stand against northern liberals. A biased jury, a judge sitting under a banner saying "Read Your Bible Daily," and an incredible outpouring of emotions marked the event.

Bryan attacked the theory of evolution as a corruption of the young, as an assault on the nobility that God had bestowed upon human beings, and as an insidious attempt by a political minority to destroy Christianity under the guise of science. Darrow, on the other hand, exposed the prejudice and ignorance of the fundamentalism that Bryan embodied. Were Adam and Eve real people? Did Joshua make the sun stand still (Josh. 10:12)? Was Jonah swallowed by a real whale? The answers to these and other questions made Bryan appear ignorant and, since he defended biblical literalism, forced him to confess that he had not read sufficiently in ancient history, philosophy, and comparative religion. In the end, the judge saved Bryan by calling an end to Darrow's cruel cross-examination. Bryan died soon after the trial, a disappointed and beaten man.

The only person who benefited from the trial was Scopes. He accepted a scholarship to the University of Chicago to study geology, a subject he researched and taught well throughout the remainder of his life. While the "monkey trial" dominated the national and international press for a few days in July 1925, it ultimately did nothing but "inherit the wind," as the title of a Hollywood movie says.

Although fundamentalism began to wane in the 1930s, it has experienced a renaissance since World War II. This has occurred within the context of a general religious awakening which has understood itself to be "evangelical" (*euangelion*, "gospel"). Sidney E. Ahlstrom suggests that the noun *evangelical* is used in America to refer to those Protestants who (1) repudiate Roman Catholicism; (2) insist on biblical literalism; (3) hold that the Bible has very serious import for Christian life; (4) stress experience and conversion over sacraments and institutions; (5) teach a legalistic rather than a situational ethic; and (6) resist fellowship with other groups who do not share their convictions.[17]

Evangelicalism links the classical fundamentalists of the nineteenth century with the fundamentalists of today. However, whereas classical fundamentalists held a strict view of biblical inerrancy that often led to a literalist view based on verbal inspiration, some popular "evangelical" biblical commentaries distinguish between inerrant theological truth and historical fact. Thus, for example, *The New Bible Dictionary* from Inter-Varsity Press is not concerned about the historical accuracy of the Book of Genesis. "Genesis has an artificial literary structure and is not concerned to provide a picture of chronological sequence but only to assert the fact that God made everything."[18] *The New Bible Commentary* of the Inter-Varsity Fellowship, published first in 1953 and constantly being revised, interprets the "six days" of creation in Genesis not as chronological days, but as "days of dramatic vision, the story being presented to Moses in a series of revelations spread over six days"; or the commentary sees "one day" as a "geological age." Similarly, the two different accounts of Jesus' ascension—Luke 24:51, which implies that the ascension happened on the same day as the resurrection and Acts 1, which postpones it for forty days—are harmonized by giving priority to Luke: "the resurrection and ascension both occurred on Easter Sunday."[19] James Barr, a recent critic of fundamentalist biblical interpretation, comments:

> The commentator . . . abandons the literary sense as soon as it would imply error or disagreement in the Bible; he achieves harmonization by taking the Acts account literally in this respect (i.e., in respect of the time of the events) and holding that the Luke account is telescoped or otherwise imprecise. Multiple ascensions form a different method of harmonization.[20]

Theologians within the evangelical movement frequently make distinctions between the "Word of God" and the Bible, affirming the inerrancy of the former but not of the latter. The Lausanne Covenant, coming out of a conference held in Switzerland (1977) on the theme of "World Evangelization," affirmed "the divine inspiration, truthfulness, and authority of both Old and New Testament Scriptures in their entirety as the only written Word of God, without error in all that it affirms, and the only infallible rule of faith and practice."[21] Theologically less careful defenders of biblical inerrancy such as Billy Graham see the Bible as only one, though the most important, instrument of God's revelation.

> The Bible is the textbook of revelation. In God's great classroom there are three textbooks—one called nature, one called conscience, and one named Scripture. The laws of God revealed in nature have never changed. In the written textbook of revelation—the Bible—God speaks through words. The Bible is the one book which reveals the Creator to the creature He created! No other book that man has conceived can make that statement and support it with fact.[22]

Since religious revival meetings have always been a part of American life in one way or another, the memories of such meetings have easily been kept alive. People remember revivalists like the ex-baseball player Billy Sunday who, together with his companion Homer A. Rodeheaver, put on a show to recruit soldiers of God who are not "hog-jowled, weasel-eyed, sponge-columned, mushy-fisted, jelly-spined, pussy-footing, four-flushing, Charlotte-russe Christians." Moreover, since the liberal Federal Council of American Churches seemed to be gaining influence, conservatives needed a united front against those who abandoned the reliable fundamentals of the faith. With the help of Billy Graham, a Presbyterian from North Carolina, a cadre of conservatives founded the National Association of Evangelicals in 1942. More radical fundamentalists joined Carl McIntyre and his organization, the American Council of Christian Churches, founded in 1941. They envisaged a fusion of the gospel and the American way of life, and they often draped the American flag over the cross to make their simple point.

After a sensational tent-meeting revival in 1949 in Los Angeles, Billy Graham became the rallying point for the evangelicals. In 1956, he formed the Billy Graham Evangelistic Association, using mass media to promote the conservative Christian cause. Carl F. H. Henry, a former professor of New Testament at Northern Baptist and Fuller Seminaries, joined the movement with his periodical *Christianity Today*. The new fundamentalists attempted to overcome the old image of fundamentalism as an anti-intellectual and antiscientific movement by arguing that the fundamental truths of Christianity were in harmony with reason and patriotism. Since its foundation in 1947, Fuller Theological Seminary in Pasadena, California, has fostered evangelical scholarship which attempts to bring harmony between the intellect, the arts, and social concerns. Bill Bright's Campus Crusade for Christ, with its secondary organizations *Youth for Christ* and *Word of Life*, tries to popularize an evangelicalism which abandons the spirit of narrow-mindedness and strife characteristic of classical fundamentalism.

There are, then, tensions between the old and the new fundamentalists. On the one hand, there are still militants who, in concert with politically conservative millionaires, crusade for conversion with slogans, uncritical biblicism, and individualistic or mass psychology. On the other hand, there are moderates such as Carl F. H. Henry who want to remain in dialogue with a pluralistic modern world. Even though the evangelical revival is no longer dominated by anti-intellectualism, hostility toward mainline denominations, and social isolation, it still echoes the classical teachings of nineteenth-century fundamentalism: the inspiration and inerrancy of the Bible, its millennial prophecy about the present as a time of trial before the Second Coming of Christ, and the need to make America the last best hope of the fundamental Christian truths which each person must accept if he or she is to be "born again" into a new life.

NOTES

1. A. C. McGiffert, *Protestant Thought Before Kant* (New York: Harper, 1962), p. 145. For a sketch of Lutheran orthodoxy, see Robert P. Scharlemann, *Thomas Aquinas and John Gerhard* (New Haven: Yale University Press, 1964), chap. 1.

2. The Lutheran Formula of Concord of 1577 intended to settle controversies among German Lutherans about the various implications for faith and morals of the doctrine of "justification by faith through grace." See "Solid Declaration" in *The Book of Concord*, ed. and trans. Theodore G. Tappert (Philadelphia: Fortress Press, 1959), pp. 466–636.

3. From the Preface of Gerhard's *Loci*, quoted in Scharlemann, *Aquinas and Gerhard*, p. 28.

4. Ibid.

5. The term is used by Sidney E. Ahlstrom, *A Religious History of the American People* (New Haven: Yale University Press, 1972), p. 366.

6. Quoted from Hodge's *Systematic Theology* (1874) in Ernest R. Sandeen, *The Roots of Fundamentalism: British and American Millenarianism, 1800-1930* (Chicago: University of Chicago Press, 1970), pp. 118-19.

7. Their detailed arguments are quoted in Sandeen, *Roots of Fundamentalism*, p. 129, from an essay on "Inspiration" in the 1881 *Presbyterian Review*.

8. For the relevant passage of the Westminster Confession, see Philip Schaff, ed., *Creeds of Christendom* (New York: Harper and Brothers, 1877), III.602:3.

9. Details in Ahlstrom, *Religious History*, p. 814, and in Ernest R. Sandeen, *The Origins of Fundamentalism: Toward a Historical Interpretation* (Philadelphia: Fortress Press, 1968), p. 22. Contrary to popular opinion, the Niagara Conference never adopted the Five Points.

10. E. J. Young, quoted in James Barr, *Fundamentalism* (London: SCM Press, 1977), p. 347 n. 24.

11. The text of the 1878 Niagara Creed is found in Appendix A of Sandeen, *Roots of Fundamentalism*, pp. 273-77.

12. The word *fundamentalist* seems to have been coined by Curtis Lee Laws in an editorial in the Northern Baptist *Watchman-Examiner*, July 1, 1920. See ibid., p. 246 n. 19.

13. This is also the thesis of the Missouri Synod historian Milton L. Rudnick, *Fundamentalism and the Missouri Synod: A Historical Study of Their Interaction and Mutual Influence* (St. Louis: Concordia Publishing House, 1966).

14. Quoted from the essay, "The Inspiration of the Bible—Definition, Extent and Proof," *The Fundamentals* (Chicago: Testimony Publishing Company, 1910-15), III.17.

15. Minutes of 26 June 1937. Quoted in Sandeen, *Roots of Fundamentalism*, p. 260.

16. For a detailed account of this crusade, see Norman F. Furniss, *The Fundamentalist Controversy, 1918-1931* (New Haven: Yale University Press, 1954), chap. 5.

17. Sidney E. Ahlstrom, "From Puritanism to Evangelicalism: A Critical Perspective" in *The Evangelicals: What They Believe, Who They Are, Where They Are Changing*, ed. David F. Wells and John D. Woodbridge (Nashville: Abingdon Press, 1975), pp. 270-71. The designation "evangelical" means "in accord with the gospel." Since Martin Luther used to describe his reform movement this way, evangelical soon came to mean

"Protestant" (from the document "Protestation," delivered by Luther's followers to the Diet of Speyer in 1529). See "Receiving Both Kinds of the Sacrament" in *Luther's Works*, American Edition, vol. 36 (Philadelphia: Fortress Press, 1959), p. 265. Protestant churches in Germany, mainly Lutheran and Reformed, are still called "evangelical" (*evangelisch*).

18. Quoted in James Barr, *Fundamentalism* (London: SCM Press, 1977), p. 41.

19. Ibid., p. 57.

20. Ibid. Barr points out that the sixteenth-century reformer Andreas Osiander used the same method of harmonization against the Bible critic Sebastian Castellio in 1545.

21. C. Rene Padilla, ed., *The New Face of Evangelicalism*, An International Symposium on the Lausanne Covenant (London: Hodder and Stoughton, 1976), p. 33.

22. Billy Graham, *How to Be Born Again* (Waco, Tex.: Word Books, 1977), pp. 39–40.

3

Fundamentalist and Biblical Authority

TWO KINDS OF GOD TALK

The real issue between fundamentalists and nonfundamentalists is not biblical literalism (who wrote what and when) but inerrancy. Fundamentalists believe that "all scripture is inspired by God" (2 Tim. 3:16) and that "no prophecy of scripture is a matter of one's own interpretation," but is instead uttered under the direct guidance of the Holy Spirit (2 Pet. 1:20–21). Fundamentalist interpreters of the Bible are not so much concerned about the historical accuracy of these two passages (whether, for example, "all scripture" means only the Old Testament) as they are about their theological inerrancy. They argue that something "inspired," be it Scripture or prophetic utterance based on Scripture, can never be false. Their interpretative (hermeneutical) key to Scripture is not the modern historical–critical method, but the rational harmonization of inspired inerrant truth with the faulty reading of sinful persons. Such harmonization rests on the assumption that biblical truth is "supernatural" even though its communication is "natural." Thus, by attempting to reconcile supernatural biblical truth with the variety of literary data, fundamentalist biblical interpreters are caught in a peculiar tension between literalism and nonliteralist harmonization.

The biblical way of talking about God is quite different from God talk in the Greek metaphysical tradition. Biblical God talk does not occur in the context of an ontological distinction of reality in which the immortal soul connects a physical and a metaphysical world. Rather, biblical God talk sees God disclosed in historical events instead of in logical or ontological operations. God declares solidarity with Israel in Egypt ("I will be your God," Exod. 6:7);

God is a warlord who helps defeat the Egyptians (Exod. 15:3); God uses unbelievers like the Assyrians to teach Israel a lesson about the covenant (Isa. 10:5, 28:21, 30:15); and God is incarnate in the person of Jesus. "When the time had fully come, God sent forth his Son . . ." (Gal. 4:4).

Whereas the Old Testament views the Exodus from Egypt and the captivity in Babylonia as the great events of God's history of salvation, leading to a blessed end sometime in the future, the New Testament regards the life, death, and resurrection of Jesus as the central event through which all other events receive meaning. Thus, while the Greek metaphysical tradition tries with dedicated sophistication to keep God in the realm of timeless immortality, the biblical tradition attests to God's radical presence in time. That is why the missionary theologian Paul called preaching Christ crucified "a folly to Gentiles" (1 Cor. 1:23). Contrary to Greek philosophical expectations, "God chose what is low and despised in the world . . . so that no human being might boast in the presence of God" (1 Cor. 1:28–29). If one has been nurtured in the Greek metaphysical tradition, this is a radical change of expectations, for that tradition teaches that there is a timeless God who can be reached through human efforts.

Some Christians have been driven into deep spiritual despair when they have attempted to appease God either through "good works," hoping for merit, or through frequent reception of metaphysical sacramental grace administered by a holy cadre of priests. When Luther, for example, experienced such despair (which he called "being attacked" or "fenced in," *Anfechtung*), he found relief in the testimonies of the prophet Habbakuk and the apostle Paul that "the righteous shall live by . . . faith" rather than by "good works" (Hab. 2:4; Rom. 1:17). If righteousness is God's gift rather than the reward for moral actions, then God is no longer perceived as a wrathful judge who must be appeased. Rather, God can be trusted as the one who has reconciled the world through Christ crucified and who relates to creatures like a father or mother to children: God loves them unconditionally, without first asking whether or not they deserve love. "I was altogether born again," Luther declared in 1545 when he recalled his experience of radical change from "works" to "faith."[1]

The biblical God is not the aloof resident of a metaphysical heaven, who is capricious in mysterious majesty. Rather, God is disclosed in the risky trust relationship embodied in the Jesus of Israel. To be hooked to this revelation, to trust its biblical story and promise, to have one's being in the living tradition of God's unconditional love in Jesus—that is the first step into the new world of eternal life. That is why a rediscovery of the gospel as the "good news" about God's incarnation in the Jesus of Israel is usually accompanied by a call to reform the church catholic—to create sufficient space for such preaching, teaching, and action so that what is said, heard, and done communicates God's unconditional love disclosed in Christ and received with childlike trust rather than a conditional love disclosed in a calculating system of credit and debit to earn salvation.

Such a call for reform does not deny that there is also a judging, wrathful God who, as Creator, insists on law and order and who rewards good and punishes evil. But the "body of Christ," the church, ought to concentrate not on the hidden God, but on the God revealed in Christ. All other concerns, though perhaps significant, tend to steer the church away from its proper function of tending the gospel in the world. In the West, given its strong tradition of metaphysical God talk, there is always the temptation to speculate about matters which may be fascinating but irrelevant. When the church father Augustine was asked, "Where was God before he created the world?" he answered, "God was creating hell for those who are inquisitive."[2] Like Doberman pinschers, alert Christians are to guard the gospel against any and all attempts to compromise it or to evade it with God talk that does not home in on the divine promise of salvation in Christ.

The language of promise has certain consequences for the way in which Christians understand their relationship to God and to each other. If I promise to love someone, I remain in open communication with the one to whom the promise is made. My life will be significantly influenced by the relationship established through such promises as, "I shall love and honor you, until death do us part." I shall find myself changing, freed for a future I may never have anticipated. I shall find that what emerges between me and the one I love is much more significant than what I see disclosed only within myself. The relationship itself will be much more authoritative than I can be as an individual. I find my identity more by being known by the other than by knowing myself, even though self-knowledge through introspection is not excluded.

Yet all human promises are conditioned by death; none of them can promise life beyond death and keep such a promise. Only God can make such a promise, and I believe that God is the Lord over life and death. Since the story of Jesus offers the promise of a future with God without death, my life may be freed from the fear of death when I trust this promise. But how do I become a believer? Only by meeting someone who communicates that promise of God's unconditional love for me in such a way that I trust him or her. That is the way in which the tradition of promise has run throughout Christian history even though there may be some extraordinary ways of communicating the promise, such as mysterious conversions which appear to occur without detectable wooing or doing between persons. God's promise of unconditional love is disclosed in the ordinary communication event of the human word, spoken and heard as well as seen and tasted in the performance of sacraments.

The point is that promise language leads to the trust in and the authority of *relationships*. There is little if any room for a Christian individualism which seeks security through either the head or the heart, that is, through dogmatic reasoning or emotional satisfaction. The language of promise opposes the language of security, which discloses a demand for control of self and of others. Concerns for security with God generally derive from a context of credit and debit: "If you do this, then you receive that." "If-then" propositions create relationships in which one partner will seek to control the other. "If you believe this, then you will be saved" or "If God is in your heart, then you will do such and such"—propositions such as these do not honor what happens *between* persons but reveal the desire to control the relationship in one way or another.

The language of promise rejects the "if-then" proposition in favor of a "because–therefore" relationship. "Because I love you, I therefore live with you until death do us part" or "because God loves me, I therefore love you as a creature of God." In this sense, one Christian defines another because the gospel emerges between people when they call on Jesus to be present. That is the promise of the "good news," and that is the business of the church, the "body of Christ" on earth.

The language of promise is kept from the pitfalls of rationalism and pious sentimentality by a realistic doctrine of sin. The Judeo-Christian tradition asserts that the human being's oldest drive for security is the desire to be like God. This is the most original sin. "You will be like God, knowing good and evil," said the serpent to Eve in the garden (Gen. 3:5). True sin, therefore, is self-deification; it is becoming like God; it is having no relationships and having power over death. "You will not die" (Gen. 3:4). Luther put it quite simply in his interpretation of the First Commandment, "You shall have no other gods":

> A god is that to which we look for all good and in which we find refuge in every time of need. To have a god is nothing else than to trust and believe him with our whole heart . . . . To have God, you see, does not mean to lay hands upon him, or put him into a purse, or shut him up in a chest. We lay hold of him when our heart embraces him and clings to him . . . . [Idolatry] concerns only that conscience which seeks help, comfort, and salvation in its own works and presumes to wrest heaven from God.[3]

That is why the proper distinction between the authority of demand and the authority of promise, between law and gospel, must be made. All human communication can be seen as a discourse which makes both demands and promises. The law always puts conditions on a relationship. "If you do this, then such and such will happen." If I drive through an intersection without obeying the stop sign, I will probably cause an accident. If I obey the sign, the accident will be prevented. Thus the law to stop before proceeding has established an ordered relationship between drivers. In this sense, it prevents the "sin" of an accident. Lutherans call this the "political" use of the law: "Let every person be subject to governing authorities" (Rom. 13:1). If I disobey the stop sign, the law reminds me that I have committed a sin against the established authority. Lutherans call this the "theological" or "pedagogical" use of the law: "through the law comes knowledge of sin" (Rom. 3:20). There is always the temptation to confuse law and gospel. I am tempted to say that the stop sign is only erected for others, not for me, and to drive through; thus I attempt to justify my selfish action. The law has then become gospel for me, the "good news" that I can do what I please. On the other hand, I could be tempted to make all others obey the laws I establish and thus make my selfish action into a tyranny for others. There are always people who want to dominate others, and there are always people who want to be dominated. In this sense, fascism is the most enduring confusion of law and gospel. The proper distinction between law and gospel is the art of making all human conditions occasions for communicating the promise of God in the Jesus of Israel.

> "God loves you for Jesus' sake." "Yes, if I could but believe that. But I can't." To which the gospel-sayer who knows his job responds, "Just by your unbelief you prove yourself to be the very man whom God loves, for he chooses above all the *un*godly!" . . . He "rightly divides law and gospel" who always finds the way to make new proposed conditions into so many objects and reasons for the promise; who in speaking of the gospel discovers how never to take "but" for an answer.[4]

There is, then, no guarantee that Christian believers will remain believers by rational, psychological, or any other means or persuasion. They are always tempted to slide back into a relationship without God. And there is always tension between the gospel, promising a future without sin, death, or evil, and the law, reminding believers of the drive to be like God.

RATIONAL NORMS AND BIBLICAL WITNESS

What, then, is the distinction between the authority of the Word of God and that of the Bible? Does the latter guarantee the former, or vice versa? Is it the work of the Holy Spirit when I become converted by reading passages of the Bible? Or are the passages themselves so inspired that they overwhelm me to the point of submitting my life to the "truth" that Jesus is resurrected and in charge of my existence? The answer to these questions depends on the kind of theological and philosophical decisions one makes concerning "authority."

If God is to be identified with the words, ideas, concepts and world views disclosed in the Bible, then the Bible is truly divine and the highest possible authority. If God is to be identified with a specific tradition, then that tradition is absolute in relation to other traditions. If God is to be identified with a particular way of thinking such as Aristotelian syllogism, then that mode of thinking leads to God. As one Roman Catholic theologian is reported to have replied to an observer who felt that there was no difference between him and a famous Anglo-Catholic: "We are the opposite pole from X. He holds every doctrine we hold, but he holds them all for the entirely irrelevant reason that he thinks them true."[5]

Those who are aware of the difference between God (who cannot be reached through any human enterprise) and mortal human existence in space and time, will not have ultimate trust in the Bible as a book. They will agree with the best ecumenical insight that God's revelation in Christ is self-authenticating. The "Word of God," which has become the code name for God's revelation, is a force in which one can participate, but which cannot be controlled. In this sense, the Word of God is end-oriented, or eschatological; its full disclosure is still in the future, in a new creation governed by the Christ who is to come as Lord of all. In the meantime, "we see in a mirror dimly" (1 Cor. 13:12).

The core of ecumenical Christianity has always affirmed the ancient ecumenical distinction between the Bible as written word and the gospel as spoken word. Whereas God's revelation through the Old and New Testaments needs to be summarized in doctrines, especially in times of crisis when the people of God are confused or persecuted, the Word of God is always a living voice, a message which creates a gathering of people held together by the speaking, hearing, and enactment of the good news of divine care for God's creatures. The gospel, therefore, gives authority to the Bible, not vice versa.

When the gospel is preserved in written form, in a "first tradition," it is authoritative in the sense that subsequent traditions can be tested to see whether they are, indeed, faithful to the gospel. In this sense, the canonical books of the Old and New Testaments have authority for those who come afterwards. These canonical writings are the norm for later creeds and doctrines, even though they may reflect different linguistic and cultural contexts. Thus, there is in Christian history a kind of hierarchy of truths and traditions, all of which are derived from and witness to God's revelation in Christ. Such a view of authority locates the Bible properly as the literary embodiment of the witness to God's revelation in

Christ, the "apostolic" witness of those who saw, heard, and spoke the Word, Christ himself. In this sense the Bible has a legal authority: it is the norm used to test Christian teachings for their faithfulness to the Word of God.

But the Bible also has a "promising" authority: the canonical writings are testimonies to the Word of God, the power that liberates one from sin, evil, and death and leads to everlasting relationships with God. The testing of doctrines is accompanied by the promise, "Thy word is a lamp to my feet and a light to my path" (Ps. 119:105). When the gospel is communicated in such a way that what is said is in conformity with what was said by the first witness, then the living Lord is heard and experienced. Thus the Bible comes alive as gospel. That is why one needs a variety of methods and tools to study and interpret it, depending upon the historical situation.

The issue is not whether biblical studies are faithful to certain doctrines, such as inerrancy or infallibility, but whether biblical study liberates the student from the straitjacket of original sin, that is, the desire to control the object of study and ultimately God, and so to become idolatrous. An honest search of the Scripture, with help from the best available tools of biblical research, will result in a realistic recognition that the Word of God in the Bible has its own self-authenticating power. The Bible receives its authority from the power of the Word of God, especially its liberating power of grace in the gospel. In and by itself the Bible has only legal power; it is a collection of religious documents which may be superior to other such documents. Those who confuse the Bible's authority of law and promise confuse creaturely humanity with divine power.

If an absent-minded professor tells me that the train for Penzance leaves Waterloo at noon, and I find in fact that it leaves Paddington one-half hour before, I do not conclude that my informant is a liar or is ill-disposed toward me or that his reputation as a scholar rests on a fraud. I take him for what he is and do not suppose that being a great authority on Homer makes him a reliable substitute for a train time-table. Similarly, Jesus Christ came into the world to be its Savior, not an authority on biblical criticism.[6]

PROPER GOSPEL COMMUNICATION

There has to be a proper distinction between a theology grounded in the Bible and a philosophy shaped by the Greek metaphysical tradition. Syllogisms and other philosophical processes are quite helpful in human interactions, especially in the areas of law and justice. But God's revelation in Jesus Christ is a story rather than an argument. Storytellers love telling the story and are not concerned with casuistic proof of the truth they want to convey. A careful distinction must be made between what God has expressly revealed in the story of the gospel and what God has not revealed. Proper gospel communication must always be on guard against the temptation to "figure out" God or to prove God's existence beyond reasonable doubt. This would be the way to control or at least to domesticate God—to have God in a box or wherever there is a gap in knowledge.

Gospel communication is quite different. It is tied to the way in which God wanted to disclose divine redeeming love: in the speaking, hearing, and enactment of the "good news" embodied in the life, work, death, and resurrection of Jesus. Ecumenical Christianity has called such gospel communication the "ministry of word and sacraments," that is, the holistic communication of God's grace. One of the ecumenical sticking-points on ministry is the fact that the communication of divine grace is tied to the externals of Word and sacraments by which Christians are called, gathered, and sent to be witnesses to Christ in the world. In other words, there must be experts in gospel communication called "ministers" who are the instrumentalists, as it were, of audible and visible communication. They are to devote their lives to gospel instrumentation by speaking, listening, teaching, baptizing, and communing. When they do this faithfully, they have done their best to achieve what God has ordained: speaking and enacting the gospel within their own existing linguistic and cultural context—for example, using the English language in the United States; using water and certain words when baptizing; and enacting the Lord's Supper by using bread and wine together with appropriate words.

When such faithful audible and visible communication occurs, the Holy Spirit, not the communicators, may bring forth faith. In this way communication of the gospel is safeguarded from a purely functionalist understanding prevalent, for example, in the medieval doctrine of "transubstantiation"—that is, when the priest speaks the words "This is my body...," the "substance" of bread and wine becomes the "substance" of Christ. While this doctrine attempts to preserve the mystery of Christ's presence in the Lord's Supper, the act of priestly consecration is so intimately linked to the mystery that the performance itself tends to be perceived as a mystery. There is a difference between the communication of the gospel and faith in the gospel. Communication itself does not guarantee faith; faith is a gift of God mediated through the Holy Spirit. Moreover, the Holy Spirit does not prefer one instrument of communication over another. There is no rivalry between the two, for both Word *and* sacraments belong to gospel communication. They are different, but not separate. God instituted both to provide a holistic communication of the gospel, for human beings, who are God's creatures, ordinarily need both.

In the enduring quarrel among Christians about the relationship between Word and sacraments, a truly ecumenical position holds that the *use* of sacraments is more important than either a completely rational understanding of them or conditions without which they cannot be effective (such as the notion that one must first believe before one can be baptized). This may be risky in view of the temptation to regard sacraments as "magic" instruments of the gospel, but faith respects the genuine mystery of divine–human communication. It is wiser to use the sacraments "rightly," that is, to administer them according to the commandment of Christ in the apostolic tradition, than to make their use dependent on other criteria—for example, baptizing without water because baptism is only a symbol of a relationship with God and the church. Sacraments communicate by the way in which they are performed, not by what is said about them. The question is, "What needs to be done so that the gospel is enacted?" What a sacrament says and what it does are not two things, but one and the same thing. Gospel communication must be holistic: the good news is spoken, heard, seen, and even tasted because that is the way in which the whole person is addressed.[7]

BY WHAT AUTHORITY?

Fundamentalists challenge nonfundamentalists to rethink the question of authority as it relates to Scripture and experience. What, for example, does it mean when Christians pledge themselves to "the prophetic and apostolic writings of the Old and New Testaments as the only true norm according to which all teachers and teachings are to be judged and evaluated"?[8] How do I know that "the Holy Spirit has called me through the Gospel, enlightened me with his gifts, and sanctified me and preserved me in true faith"?[9]

There is a deep ecumenical conviction that the authority of Christ is in the "word," that is, in the communication event between persons. Although "God is spirit" (John 4:24), God is also a person, Jesus Christ, using ordinary means of communication. Thus the Word of God comes alive when it is spoken by one person to another. The Word is not separated from the Holy Spirit. The New Testament affirms this unity of Word and Spirit in a variety of ways: rebirth is effected through water and Spirit in baptism (John 3:5; Titus 3:5); Christ is present in the letter which is written "with the Spirit of the living God," who is with those who preach (2 Cor. 3:3–8); the Holy Spirit creates true thanksgiving with psalms, hymns, and prayers (Eph. 5:18–21); the Spirit is in the words of those who proclaim Christ after his departure from the world (John 14:26); and the deeds and life style of Christians in the world are empowered by the Holy Spirit, "for the kingdom of God does not consist in talk but in power" (1 Cor. 4:20).

Authority (*auctoritas*, "origins") emerges in relationships having the same roots. The relationship between a judge and a defendant, for example, is rooted in the community of law which applies its norms to both judge and defendant. Every Christian, no matter what position he or she occupies in a human hierarchy, is rooted in the gospel, that is, in the good news that Christ brought about reconciliation between God and sinful creatures. Christ, therefore, bestows authority to the Bible, to tradition, to the church, and to individuals. His authority must be constantly rediscovered in a world filled with competing claims of authority. That is why the church must be constantly "re-formed," that is, it must be reminded of and brought back to the authority of Christ.

Among Christians, there has to be a kind of therapeutic conflict, as it were, as to whether or not Christ is the focus of what is called "gospel." But a clear distinction must be made between needless contention and necessary controversy. When the Word of God is discerned and embodied in the church, the body of Christ, true freedom has come into being—the freedom *for* God and *from* the world, though never a complete and perfect freedom. Life in the world is still affected by sin, death, and evil; yet the die has been cast, and Christ's disciples know their ultimate destiny. In this sense, authority emerges in the communication event of "gospeling": I am addressed in my fears and hopes by the good news that my salvation is in Christ rather than in myself.

Since God has been disclosed in the person of Jesus, knowledge of God does not consist of transcending rational truths, nor is it communicated through special spiritual experiences. Neither the Bible nor individual gifts of the Holy Spirit are so authoritative as to bypass the event of human communication in its holistic way of speaking, hearing, and doing. One can always assume that God could have found better ways of disclosing the divine being, but this is nevertheless the way God chose. God is known only through revelation; and God's decisive revelation occurred in the Jesus of Israel, whose real historicity is difficult to establish and whose gospel is burdened by the complexities of human communication.

The real presence of Christ is tied to the struggle for clarity in human communication. There may be times when such clarity is given suddenly and without apparent struggle, as was the case at the "birth" of the church in Jerusalem at Pentecost. But those who yearn for the same experience today should remember that before and after Pentecost the disciples of Jesus had to go through (rather than around) the struggle of human communication. There was anxiety in the "upper room" (Acts 1:13), and during the persecution (Acts 4:3).

We need to learn to appreciate the fundamentalist search for rational truth and the charismatic experience of simple joy, but those who boast of being born again must be reminded that certainty is plagued by doubt, joy is dampened by anxiety, and life with Christ is always cruciform.

NOTES

1. "Preface to the Complete Edition of Luther's Latin Writings, 1545" in *Luther's Works*, American Edition, vol. 34 (Philadelphia: Fortress Press, 1960), p. 337.

2. Quoted by Luther in "Table Talk," in *Luther's Works*, American Edition, vol. 54 (Philadelphia: Fortress Press, 1967), p. 377.

3. "The Large Catechism," in *The Book of Concord*, ed. Theodore G. Tappert (Philadelphia: Fortress Press, 1959), pp. 365:2, 366:13–15, 367:22.

4. Eric W. Gritsch and Robert W. Jenson, *Lutheranism: The Theological Movement and Its Confessional Writings* (Philadelphia: Fortress Press, 1976), p. 44.

5. P. T. Forsythe, *The Faith of a Moralist* (London: Macmillan, 1930), p. 198.

6. John Huxtable, *The Bible Says* (London: SCM Press, 1962), p. 170.

7. For a pioneering analysis of audible and visible gospel communication, see Robert W. Jenson, *Visible Words: The Interpretation and Practice of Christian Sacraments* (Philadelphia: Fortress Press, 1978), especially part I.

8. "Formula of Concord," in *The Book of Concord*, pp. 503–504:3.

9. "The Small Catechism," Article III (The Creed), in ibid., p. 345:6.

4

The Charismatic Movement

CHARISMATIC PHENOMENA

In both Judaism and Christianity there have always been people who experienced God in a special way; they have been called "charismatics" (from the Greek word *charisma*, "gift of grace"). The Old Testament speaks of a variety of charismatics. Some received special powers to rule over the people of Israel. King Saul, for example, was "turned into another man" by the Spirit of God (1 Sam. 10:6). Others received the power over life and death: the prophet Elijah resurrected a child from the dead by stretching his body over the corpse and praying to God for the return of life (1 Kings 17:21). God inspired priests from the tribe of Levi to make military and political judgments (2 Chron. 20:14–17), and the temple musicians were a significant component of inspired prophecy (1 Chron. 25:1).

There was an ardent expectation of a messianic king who would establish eternal peace because "the Spirit of the Lord shall rest upon him" (Isa. 11:1–2; 42:1). God employed kings, prophets, and priests to create and maintain justice, wisdom, and true worship. God even employed a "lying spirit" in the mouth of prophets to entice a disobedient King Ahab to change his mind (1 Kings 22:21–28).

The first Christians regarded reception of the Holy Spirit as the sign of God's work to bring people back into proper relationship with their Creator. John the Baptist declared that the Jewish prophecy of a messianic king was fulfilled in Jesus of Nazareth, who baptized not with water, but with the Holy Spirit (Mark 1:8). Johannine and Pauline writings describe the Holy Spirit as the driving force of the Christian community during the interim between the resurrection of Jesus and his return at the end of time. The Holy Spirit is the "counselor" (*parakletos*) who, as the "spirit of truth," was with the disciples in their mission on earth (John

14:16); God has given the Spirit to the church as a "guarantee" (*arrabon*, a credit or pledge for the future); and every believer participates in the new eternal life by being "born of water and the Spirit" (John 3:5).

The Holy Spirit changed frightened disciples into effective missionaries through noise, wind, and tongues of fire (Acts 2:1–4). Fifty days after the resurrection of Jesus, during the harvest festival in Jerusalem, the disciples moved from the "upper room" into the streets, miraculously proclaiming the gospel in many languages to people from various parts of the Roman Empire (Acts 2:9–11). This is the charismatic phenomenon known as "xenolalia" (*xenos*, "foreign," and *lalein*, "to babble" or "to speak"). The day is known as Pentecost (*pentekoste*, "the fiftieth day") and has subsequently been celebrated as the birthday of the Christian church. Some later Christians spoke not only foreign languages with no previous training but also a strange tongue which no one understood—a charismatic phenomenon known as "glossolalia" *(glossa*, "tongue," and *lalein*). People who practice glossolalia are frequently ecstatic; they utter strange melodic or unmelodic sounds and experience feelings of joy.

When the phenomenon surfaced in Corinth, the apostle Paul presented the congregation with a sober assessment of the meaning of *charisma*. He explained that it denoted a variety of things: salvation (Rom. 5:15; 1 Cor. 1:11), specific functions in the church (1 Cor. 12:28), and even celibacy, which Paul recommended in 1 Cor. 7:7. At the beginning of his more systematic treatment of gifts, Paul listed the charismata in the context of other "inspired" phenomena in the church such as "service" and "working" (1 Cor. 12:4). Moreover, the apostle described believers as "pneumatics," that is, persons who have received the Holy Spirit and are thus "spiritual" —which makes every Christian a charismatic in this sense (1 Cor. 3:1; Gal. 6:1).

But Paul had no desire to single out unique gifts. Teaching and exhortation are "charismata" (Rom. 12:7–8; 15:14); the self-control mentioned as a fruit of the Spirit in Gal. 5:23 becomes a gift of the Spirit in 1 Cor. 7:7 when it is applied to self-control in sexual matters; love (*agape* in Greek) is a "more excellent way" than gifts (1 Cor. 12:31).

Thus Paul acknowledged the experiencing of special powers through the Holy Spirit, such as speaking in tongues, provided that the whole community was thereby edified and the "common good" was served (1 Cor. 14:39–40). He admonished the Corinthians not to be fascinated with extraordinary ecstatic powers which pagans admire. Rather, they ought to understand special gifts and the individuation of the greatest gift of all, Jesus Christ, who calls people to service and to witness in a fallen world.

Paul's disciples, therefore, had no difficulty associating the commission for ministry—ordination by the laying on of hands—with a gift of the Spirit (1 Tim. 4:14) which was shared by all "as good stewards of God's varied grace" (1 Pet. 4:10). Paul and the leaders of the first Christian congregations considered extraordinary experiences ("signs and wonders") subordinate to the central proclamation of salvation through Christ crucified. "I decided to know nothing among you except Jesus Christ and him crucified," Paul told the Corinthians (1 Cor. 2:2), "for Jews demand signs and Greeks seek wisdom, but we preach Christ crucified, a stumbling block to Jews and a folly to Gentiles" (1 Cor. 1:22–23). Weakness, suffering, and death are more significant than miracles or extraordinary spiritual power (1 Cor. 2:3–4; 12:9–10; Phil. 3:10).

There is always the probability that a false satanic spirit is at work in the experiencing of triumphant spiritual power (2 Cor. 11:13–15). When Christians discern the imminent end of the world, their discernment may be an illusion. "The coming of the lawless one by the activity of Satan will be with all power and with pretended signs and wonders . . . [to those who] refused to love the truth and so be saved . . . . God sends upon them a strong delusion, to make them believe what is false" (2 Thess. 2:9–11).

First Corinthians 12–14 is Paul's pastoral attempt to integrate manifested gifts of the Spirit into the Corinthian congregation's common task to be disciples of the Christ, who calls for cruciform service in the world. As disciples, the Corinthians must stay alert and "test" the gifts. "For God is not a God of confusion but of peace" (1 Cor. 14:33). While there may be differences in the Christian community, these differences are not to divide but rather to strengthen its members to fulfill their calling in the world. The variety of gifts ought to lead to a common witness, manifested in ethical behavior (Romans 12–14). Ultimately, disciples of Christ are "little Christs" to their neighbors. "We who are strong ought to bear with the failings of the weak, and not to please ourselves; . . . let each of us please his neighbor for his good, to edify him. For Christ did not please himself" (Rom. 15:1–3).

The charismatic phenomena of xenolalia and glossolalia have been singled out by some Christian groups as the essential marks of a Christian. These groups, who understand themselves as "pentecostal," argue that the true church always receives the gift of "tongues," accompanied by the power of healing and other manifestations, to mark the difference between worldly and otherworldly existence. A paradigmatic example of such a group is the Montanist movement of the second century, named after the Asia Minor prophet Montanus.

Montanus and his two prophetesses, Priscilla and Maximilla, in millennialist fashion believed that the world would end during their lifetime; that believers should assemble at a specific place to await the end; and that strict fasting, complete abstinence from sexual activity, and readiness for martyrdom should characterize true believers. Montanism gained popular support throughout the Roman Empire until A.D. 179, when Maximilla died without having experienced the Second Coming of Christ she had predicted. Similar movements have appeared in subsequent centuries, although they have not always been as radical as Montanism in their teaching and behavior. Among these are the Society of Friends, nicknamed Quakers by their foes, and the United Society of Believers in Christ's Second Coming, known as Shakers.

Defenders of pentecostalism and others interested in the history of Christian "enthusiasm" (*entheos*, "filled with God," "in God") see in the Quakers and Shakers a living link between ancient and modern charismatics.[1] Although the Quakers, under the leadership of George Fox, exhibited a few Montanist features in the 1650s, they soon became known for their belief in the "inner light" or "spark" to be found in every human creature, a spark which is the basis of a mystical community of charity for all.

The Shakers, on the other hand, did exhibit classic Montanist features. In 1774, they moved from Manchester, England, to the vicinity of Albany, New York, and founded a commune under the leadership of their prophetess Ann Lee Stanley. They abstained completely from sexual activity, convinced that the union of Adam and Eve was the root of all evil; they regarded glossolalia as a sign of true faith and the indication that Christ's Second Coming was imminent; and they practiced a peculiar form of religious dancing. Ann Lee Stanley died in 1784, but the Shakers continued to be successful in making converts and in founding several communes in New England, Ohio, and Kentucky between 1830 and 1850.

THE PENTECOSTAL REVIVAL

An unusual event occurred during the vigil on December 31, 1900, at Bethel College in Topeka, Kansas, where forty students had assembled in prayer under the leadership of evangelist Charles F. Parham. Parham had left the Methodist church in 1895 to search for a meaningful charismatic experience to meet the challenges of the new twentieth century. He had founded the college, developed a curriculum around its only textbook, the Bible, and focused on the study of the phenomenon of "baptism by the Holy Spirit."

During this vigil, Parham laid hands on Agnes N. Ozman, one of the students who had requested to receive the Holy Spirit, and she not only spoke in tongues, praising God, but talked in several foreign languages as well, including Chinese. "It was as though rivers of living water were proceeding from my innermost being," Agnes later confessed.[2] Those present claimed to have seen a halo around her head and face. Many joined her in speaking foreign tongues as well as making sounds which were not discernible as communicative language. Newspapers such as *The Kansas City Times* reported that twenty-one languages had been spoken during that service and in subsequent revival meetings.

Parham concluded that it would no longer be necessary for missionaries to learn foreign languages. Instead, baptism by the Holy Spirit would be the only requirement for a missionary, since it would provide the missionary with the ability to speak any language needed to communicate the gospel. In 1901, Parham closed Bethel College and held revival meetings in Kansas and Missouri. In 1905, he founded a Bible Training School in Houston, Texas, with an enrollment of twenty-five students who were to be the new missionaries of the pentecostal revival. Revival meetings in Houston drew large crowds, and observers reported the occurrence of visions, glossolalia, xenolalia, and healings.

Among Parham's Houston students was William J. Seymour, a black man from Louisiana, who was eager to be trained in Bible study. Although segregation laws prohibited the mixing of whites and blacks, Parham admitted Seymour because of his strong desire to learn. Seymour did not speak in tongues while in Houston, but he was deeply impressed by those who did, particularly Neely Terry, a black woman and member of a small holiness church in Los Angeles which had defected from the Negro Baptist Church. A Mrs. Hutchinson had been elected to act as pastor of the small group of defectors, but Miss Neely thought that Seymour would be a good candidate for the position.

In 1906, Seymour accepted the position in Los Angeles after visiting and conducting several holiness revivals along the way. When he preached his first sermon, with Acts 2:4 as a text, arguing that true believers must speak in tongues even though he himself could not, Mrs. Hutchinson refused to let him use the church. Since most of the members of the church agreed with Seymour, he had no difficulty finding shelter in a member's home, where he prayed, studied, and meditated until he, together with seven others, spoke in strange tongues on the night of April 6, 1906.

Curious crowds soon assembled whenever Seymour preached. He moved to an abandoned Methodist church at 312 Azusa Street, where he continued to attract larger and larger crowds of mixed races. The "Holy Rollers" of Azusa Street were soon known all over the city and, after being featured in the *Los Angeles Times*, became a tourist attraction. When the infamous earthquake struck San Francisco on April 18, 1906, Seymour and his pentecostal disciples saw it as a sign of perdition for those who refused to repent.

Thousands of people flocked to the Azusa Mission from all over the United States. Seymour and his staff lived on the upper floor, known as "the pentecostal upper room," and were visited by people who desired a charismatic experience. People of all races were welcomed, money poured in, and hundreds of preachers from various denominations made pilgrimages to Azusa Street either to observe or to be converted to the pentecostal cause. When Charles Parham, Seymour's teacher, visited Los Angeles in 1906 and tried to curb the frenzy of the meetings, Seymour's disciples refused to let him stay. Though Parham subsequently denounced the Azusa mission as a form of spiritual prostitution, the movement continued, spreading to the far West and South, to New York, and even abroad.

Oslo, Norway, became the first pentecostal center in Europe after the Norwegian Methodist pastor, T. B. Barratt, on a tour of the United States, had received the gift of tongues at a November 1906 revival meeting in New York. Until his death in 1940, Barratt nurtured the pentecostal movement, which by then had reached virtually every European country.[3]

The 1906 Los Angeles revival represented the birth of the modern pentecostal movement. Its basic theological stance was briefly stated in the first issue of Seymour's periodical, *The Apostolic Faith*, published in 1906 and sent free of charge to thousands of people, especially in the South. Describing the pentecostal revival as "the apostolic faith movement," the periodical listed as essential pentecostal teachings: repentance, confession of sins, and faith in Christ, which consisted of "two works." The first work was "justification," that is, the "act of God's free grace by which we receive remission of sins." The second work was "sanctification," that is, the "act of God's free grace by which He makes us holy." To be cleansed from sin was the prerequisite for baptism by the Holy Spirit. "Jesus cleansed and got all doubt out of His Church before He went back to glory." The second work was crowned by baptism by the Holy Spirit, marked by speaking in tongues, as with the disciples on the day of Pentecost. Finally, there was divine healing. The pentecostal believer "must believe that God is able to heal."[4]

From its very beginnings, however, Seymour's Azusa Mission was opposed by those who refused to regard the charismatic phenomenon of speaking in tongues as an essential mark of Christian life. The Church of the Nazarene, whose founding congregation was in Los Angeles before its incorporation into a denomination in 1908, became the center of the opposition. Members of the denomination defended the Wesleyan theology of sanctification as the second work (after justification) which nurtures believers in the growth of grace but which does not totally eliminate the inherited sin of Adam—"original sin" and "the residue of sin within," as Wesley had called it. Seymour's disciples taught that sanctification cleansed believers even of original sin through baptism by the Holy Spirit, and many pentecostal Baptists shared this view, claiming that conversion and baptism with the Holy Spirit completed Christ's work of atonement.

W. H. Durham, pastor of Chicago's North Avenue Mission and a disciple of Seymour's, became the leader of pentecostals who held the "finished-work theory": there is no need for any further change after conversion because baptism with the Holy Spirit finishes the atonement begun by Christ and makes believers "perfect." That is, Spirit baptism cleanses them from all sin, including the original sin inherited from Adam and Even through birth.

What was at stake in this controversy was the enduring theological problem of the relationship between sin and grace. St. Augustine had already struggled with the British monk Pelagius over this relationship. Augustine taught that believers will always have a residue of sin in them and are thus unable freely to choose their salvation; they are chosen by God's free grace rather than by their own free will. Pelagius, on the other hand, taught that believers are unaffected by the sin of Adam and are able to choose whether or not to be with God; they are totally free to say yes or no to the salvation offered through the gospel of Jesus. Augustine, Luther, Wesley, and other theologians represented the generally accepted view that, as Luther put it, believers are "simultaneously sinful and righteous." Absolute perfection is experienced only after the final judgment at the end of time, when God's final rule in a new creation has been established.

Seymour's disciples, W. H. Durham and Eudorus N. Bell (the latter was editor of *Word and Witness* of Malvern, Kansas), attempted to coordinate various radical views on such issues as sin, grace, and millennialism. Bell was finally charged with developing organizational structures, and did so by calling "all saints who believe in baptism with the Holy Ghost" to an April 1914 meeting in Hot Springs, Arkansas, to coordinate the radical pentecostal movement. Three hundred delegates from all over the United States assembled and quickly adopted a preamble and a polity which gave local groups autonomy and assigned coordinating leaders to an executive agency.

The new organization called itself the Assemblies of God and established its headquarters in Findlay, Ohio. Organization leaders issued a Statement of Faith, which affirmed speaking in tongues and the teaching that "entire sanctification" is "progressive" rather than "instantaneous." This latter view cooled down pentecostalism's most radical assertion that baptism by the Holy Spirit is the "finished work of Christ" and left the door open for a future union between Methodist moderates, represented by the Churches of the Nazarene, and Baptist radicals, united in the Assemblies of God.

Although the Assemblies of God managed to unite the defenders of the finished-work theory, members of the new organization were soon plagued by another controversy about Christ's place in the Trinity, known as the "Jesus only" or "pentecostal unitarian" issue. The controversy began during a baptismal service at an international camp meeting in Los Angeles in 1913, when a speaker claimed that the apostles baptized only in the name of Jesus and did not use the phrase "in the name of the Father and of the Son and of the Holy Spirit."

One of the attending pastors, Frank Ewart, a native of Australia and a leading figure in the West Coast pentecostal movement, pursued the question and concluded that there was only one person in the Godhead, namely Jesus, and that the names "Father" and "Holy Spirit" were only titles to designate various aspects of Christ. The doctrine of the Trinity, Ewart argued, was an invention of the bishop of Rome who persuaded the Council of Nicea to adopt it in A.D. 325; thus the Nicene Creed is irrelevant. After 1914, Ewart rebaptized everyone who agreed with him—in the name of Jesus only. In 1916, the general council of the Assemblies of God ousted the pentecostal unitarians, who then organized into the Pentecostal Assemblies of the World. The latter became the United Pentecostal Church in 1945, which comprised a large number of "oneness" churches.

Once again an enduring theological problem had divided pentecostalism: the relationship between Jesus of Nazareth and God, between the humanity and the divinity of Christ. The Egyptian theologian Arius had already struggled with this question in the fourth century, concluding that Christ was a creature who was subordinated to rather than equal with God. When Arius was excommunicated for this heresy by the Synod of Alexandria (A.D. 318), various controversies ensued, leading to the trinitarian creed of Nicea in 325. Still, the christological quarrels lasted until A.D. 451, when the Council of Chalcedon affirmed the traditional doctrine of the Trinity as normative for the church. The Assemblies of God reaffirmed that doctrine in their 1916 Statement of Fundamental Truths, thus aligning themselves with ecumenical orthodoxy and rejecting unitarianism in general.

One of the most controversial pentecostal revivalists was Aimee Elizabeth Semple McPherson, known as "Sister Aimee" by her followers. Sister Aimee was born in Canada, grew up a Methodist, and received baptism by the Holy Spirit in 1908 during a revival conducted by the evangelist Robert Semple, whom she married shortly afterwards. Both went on an evangelism tour of Canada and the United States and joined the Assemblies of God in Findlay, Ohio. In 1910 they were sent as missionaries to China, where Robert Semple was stricken with malaria and died shortly after their arrival.

Hardly twenty years old and the mother of a baby, Aimee returned to the United States and married Harold McPherson, a salesman for a New England wholesale grocery firm. When her husband refused to accompany her on her revival tours, she left him in 1917 and, with her newborn son from that marriage, went to Los Angeles and organized the Echo Park Evangelistic Association. In 1922 she was ordained as a Baptist preacher and, using her experience as an actress in high school, attracted large crowds of followers who helped her build the magnificent Angelus Temple.

After 1927, her organization was called The International Church of the Foursquare Gospel. The name was derived from Ezek. 1:1–28, with its vision of four angelic creatures—a man, a lion, an ox, and an eagle. Sister Aimee, in a sermon preached in 1921 in Oakland, revealed that the vision of the four creatures inspired her to create a denomination. As she put it:

> A perfect gospel! A complete gospel for body, for soul, for spirit, and for eternity. A gospel that faces squarely in every direction . . . . In my soul was born a harmony that struck and sustained upon four full, quivering strings, and from it were plucked words that leaped into being—THE FOURSQUARE GOSPEL.[5]

In a *Declaration of Faith*, Sister Aimee presented twenty-two articles which were derived largely from her theological reflections published in several earlier books, especially *The Foursquare Gospel*. A monthly periodical, *The Bridal Call*, and a weekly newspaper, the *Crusader*, stressed sanctification, baptism by the Holy Spirit, divine healing, and the Second Coming of Christ. Baptism by the Holy Spirit was the center of all her teachings. Mrs. McPherson also broadcast these teachings through the medium of the first known church radio station in Los Angeles, which was associated with the Angelus Temple.

In 1931, Sister Aimee married a third time, this time to a singer named David Hutton. She died in 1944 from an overdose of Seconal, a "harmless sedative" according to news media. Her funeral was a lavish affair, photographed by *Life* magazine. Rolf K. McPherson, a son from her second marriage, presided over the denomination after Sister Aimee's death.

The holiness revival in America was rooted in millennial hope and in the Wesleyan doctrine of perfection. In 1949, the pentecostal movement organized its own World Pentecostal Fellowship in Paris, France, in opposition to the World Council of Churches (organized in 1948). A majority of pentecostal churches also joined the National Association of Evangelicals. The North American Fellowship, linked to the World Pentecostal Fellowship, continues to represent churches from Canada and the United States.

There has been a growing ecumenical spirit among pentecostals since World War II. David Du Plessis, one of the movement's most influential leaders and secretary of the 1952 Pentecostal World Conference, urged member churches attending the conference to forgo their "ostracism" because "they have something to gain by larger fellowship with all who truly belong to Christ."[6] The well-known pentecostal preacher Oral Roberts became a Methodist in 1965. Some pentecostal groups still insist on speaking in tongues, be it glossolalia or xenolalia, while others do not. But the ecumenical pentecostal spirit is still intimately linked to a strong belief in Spirit baptism as the most characteristic feature of pentecostalism.

THE NEW CHARISMATICS

When pentecostals began to share their religious experiences with other Christians in the 1950s, many nonpentecostals were attracted to the movement. Oral Roberts and a wealthy dairyman from California, Demos Shakarian, organized the Full Gospel Business Men's Fellowship International (FGBMFI) in Los Angeles to facilitate communication between business leaders who had been baptized by the Holy Spirit. In 1953, the FGBMFI started publishing a monthly magazine, *The Voice*, which informed its local, national, and international chapters of various pentecostal events. *The Voice* was also distributed to many members of the clergy and laity of mainline denominations. In addition, David Du Plessis, an ordained minister of the Assemblies of God and a man respected in ecumenical circles as "Mr. Pentecost," lectured and traveled widely among nonpentecostals. Protestant ecumenical leaders recognized pentecostalism as a "third force" in modern Christendom, in addition to Roman Catholicism and Protestantism.

Recognition of pentecostalism as a respectable component of ecumenical Christianity was accompanied by an outbreak of speaking in tongues at St. Mark's Episcopal Church in Van Nuys, California, in the 1960s. The rector of St. Mark's, Dennis Bennett, was a native of London who had been raised in a Congregationalist parsonage and who had converted to the Episcopal church in 1951 after completing his theological studies at the University of Chicago Divinity School. When he accepted the call to St. Mark's in 1953, he was a supporter of the Anglo-Catholic wing of the Episcopal church. By 1960, he was known as a successful pastor who had increased St. Mark's membership from five hundred to twenty-five hundred through excellent pastoral care and financial stewardship.

Then, in November 1959, Bennett received the baptism by the Holy Spirit during a prayer meeting with a friend and fellow pastor, Frank Maguire, in the latter's parish. This prayer meeting had been organized by members of Bennett's parish, John and Joan Baker, who had experienced baptism by the Spirit during a meeting with pentecostal friends, but who had remained Episcopalians. Indeed, they were better Episcopalians; they attended all services, tithed, and shared their experience with other members, some of whom also began to speak in tongues.

Soon eight pastors and about one hundred lay people, including seventy members of St. Mark's, experienced glossolalia. Rumors spread throughout the city of Van Nuys that St. Mark's had become a center of Holy Rollers, a phenomenon not usually associated with Episcopalians. Although charismatic meetings often lasted beyond midnight, they were never disorderly.

Father Bennett tried to explain the activities of the charismatic group in his 1960 Palm Sunday sermon. Most of his parishioners, however, refused to tolerate his views and activities. One of the curates resigned, and the parish treasurer asked Bennett also to resign. Bennett did so within two days, explaining his action in a lengthy pastoral letter which contained a declaration that he would not leave the Episcopalian priesthood. Francis Bloy, bishop of the Los Angeles diocese and Bennett's superior, prohibited speaking in tongues, but the story of charismatic activities at St. Mark's received public attention in the summer 1960 issues of *Time* and *Newsweek* magazines. Bennett was subsequently branded a fanatic and a crank by many rank-and-file Episcopalians.

In July 1960, the bishop of Olympia, Washington, called Bennett to St. Luke's Episcopal Church in Seattle. At that time St. Luke's had two hundred apathetic members and was financially bankrupt. One year later, eighty members of the parish had received baptism with the Holy Spirit, all debts were paid, and the budget was increased. By 1968, two thousand worshipers attended St. Luke's services every week. Father Bennett was now the acknowledged leader of a new charismatic movement which had begun to penetrate not only Episcopalian, but also Presbyterian, Lutheran, and Roman Catholic churches.

An early lay leader of the new charismatic movement was Jean Stone, a member of St. Mark's in Van Nuys. An affluent housewife married to a director of the Lockheed Aircraft Company, she had felt useless in the Episcopalian church until she was baptized by the Holy Spirit at a prayer meeting at St. Mark's in 1960. In 1961, after Father Bennett left, she organized the Blessed Trinity Society to emphasize the work of the third person of the Trinity. The society's meetings stressed prayer fellowship, teaching "Christian Advance" seminars, and evangelism. The literary voice of the society was *Trinity*, a quarterly periodical financed in large measure by Jean's husband Donald. By 1963, the society had attracted fifty-nine patrons who contributed one hundred dollars each, and nine sponsors who had given at least one thousand dollars each. David Du Plessis became a member of the board of directors and Ralph

Wilkerson, an Assemblies of God minister who later headed the Melodyland Christian Center in Anaheim, helped Jean Stone form the "Christian Advance" seminars, known after 1967 as "charismatic clinics." The seminars became the seedbed for charismatic conferences which featured pentecostal testimonies, Bible study, and glossolalia.

In 1966, after Jean Stone divorced her husband and married an editor of *Trinity*, leaving with him to become "faith missionaries" for the new charismatic movement in Hong Kong, the Blessed Trinity Society was absorbed by Melodyland. *Trinity* was replaced by the *Logos Journal*, published in Plainfield, New Jersey, and by the *New Covenant*, issued in Ann Arbor, Michigan, after 1971. These became the two leading periodicals of the movement.

The charismatic movement spread rapidly in the 1960s with the help of the news media. Harold Bredesen, pastor of the First Reformed Church in Mt. Vernon, New York, was one of several leaders who lectured at Inter-Varsity Christian Fellowship meetings on college campuses. At one meeting at Yale, Episcopalian, Lutheran, Presbyterian, Methodist, and Roman Catholic students spoke in tongues. From these "GlossoYalies," as they were nicknamed, the movement spread to Dartmouth College, Stanford University, Princeton Theological Seminary, and a number of other colleges and seminaries in the northeastern, northcentral, and far western states.

In England, the distribution of *Trinity* magazine and visits by Father Frank Maguire in 1963 helped establish a fledgling charismatic movement there. Michael Harper, until then the rector of All Souls Church, Langham Palace, London, became the movement's leader in 1964. He and other British charismatics created the organization Fountain Trust (named after the Fountain Gate in Jerusalem and illustrative of the work of the Holy Spirit) and *Renewal* magazine. Fountain Trust has no membership rules and is sustained by voluntary contributions. Harper wanted those who experienced baptism by the Holy Spirit to stay in their respective churches in order to renew them.

Fountain Trust's doctrinal platform stresses four objectives: (1) to be "Christ centered," that is, to see the work of the Spirit as the glorification of Christ, who is the source of all renewal; (2) to be "charismatic" in the sense of remaining ecumenical, that is, to see the work of the Spirit as a unifying force in the church universal; (3) to be "corporate" and not individualistic by recognizing that the Spirit always creates communal relationships; and (4) to be "compassionate," that is, to see love as the heart of renewal, which discloses itself in evangelism and social action.[7]

The first charismatic renewal conference based on this platform was held in London in 1965 and was linked to a FGBMFI convention that united American and British charismatic leaders. Widely publicized by the news media, the conference concluded with an address by Oral Roberts at the Royal Albert Hall in London.

The new charismatic movement began to penetrate Roman Catholicism in 1966, when several lay faculty members of Duquesne University in Pittsburgh held prayer meetings to renew their active membership in the church. They also read David Wilkerson's 1964 best seller, *The Cross and the Switchblade*, which, after relating the author's work among young drug addicts in New York City, concluded with an account of his pentecostal experience. The group also visited charismatic prayer meetings in Pittsburgh. At one such meeting, Ralph Keifer, an instructor in the Duquesne department of theology, prayed for the reception of the Holy Spirit and received the gift of glossolalia. A student–faculty retreat, later known as the "Duquesne weekend," was held in February 1967, and at this event about thirty people were baptized by the Holy Spirit.

With this charismatic cadre as a nucleus, the movement spread to the University of Notre Dame and to Michigan State University. The charismatic university groups met with local chapters of the FGBMFI, and, by the summer of 1967, more than three thousand charismatics—most of them priests, nuns, and teaching monks— attended a "Notre Dame weekend." Since then, the annual Catholic pentecostal conferences at Notre Dame have attracted thousands of people (thirty thousand in 1974) from all over the world. Ten thousand delegates from fifty countries at the 1975 international conference in Rome heard Pope Paul VI call the charismatic movement a chance for renewal in the church. Several Roman Catholic bishops have supported the movement, including Leo Cardinal Suenens, primate of Belgium, who initiated the pastoral guidelines which advocate cooperation between "enthusiasm and institution."[8]

In the 1960s, Lutheran pastors started a Lutheran charismatic movement[9] led by Larry Christenson, a clergyman of the American Lutheran Church (ALC) and pastor of Trinity Lutheran Church, San Pedro, California. One year after his call to Trinity, Christenson and his wife experienced speaking in tongues, an event which caused controversy in his congregation.

In 1963, the South Pacific District Convention of the ALC issued "guidelines" which discouraged glossolalia on the basis of 1 Corinthians 12–14. The guidelines recommended that glossolalia be confined to private devotional life and that clergy and laity not participate in meetings which encourage speaking in tongues. Charismatic members of Trinity rejected the guidelines as unscriptural on the basis of 1 Cor. 14:39, "earnestly desire to prophesy, and do not forbid speaking in tongues." When some members wanted to break away from the ALC, Pastor Christenson offered to resign. His offer was turned down at a congregational meeting; forty members subsequently left the congregation, and Trinity remained with the ALC.

Bible study and prayer meetings marked by charismatic events continued. At one time, after deliberations about constructing an addition to the church building, an unmarked envelope containing $25,000 in cash appeared in Pastor Christenson's study. At another time, a request for organizational restructuring of the congregation emerged from prayer meetings, and four elders were commissioned to extend the work of the pastor through counseling, assisting at worship, visitations, and other pastoral acts. A bookstore to disseminate charismatic literature was set up. Christenson himself wrote a number of charismatic books.[10]

Since the organizing of the Minneapolis International Lutheran Conference on the Holy Spirit in 1972, the Lutheran charismatic movement has moved far beyond parochial boundaries. Conferences now feature speakers such as David Du Plessis and David Wilkerson, who represent the worldwide movement; workshops deal with almost any topic, especially prayer, worship, and morals; a variety of people give testimonials about glossolalia and healings.

Regional organizations continue the work of the international conference. Midwestern Lutheran charismatics are organized in the Lutheran Charismatic Renewal of Valparaiso, Indiana. The organization provides a variety of information through its "Paraclete

Communication Service," which distributes filmstrips, literature, and other material. Another regional organization is Lutheran Charisciples in Portland, Oregon. This organization began to operate in 1971, and its members understand themselves to be "Lutheran Christians who are seriously seeking to walk with Christ-the-Lord in the 'light' of God's Word and under the 'baptism' of, in, with the Holy Spirit . . . to witness to the Charismatic Christ in these last days of God's patient grace."[11] Although discouraged by Lutheran denominational leaders, the Lutheran Charisciples, calling for healing services and speaking in tongues, have succeeded in penetrating many Lutheran congregations.

The three major Lutheran church bodies in the United States—the ALC, the Lutheran Church in America (LCA) and The Lutheran Church–Missouri Synod (LCMS)—have attempted to deal with the Lutheran charismatic movement in a variety of ways.[12] In a 1964 "Statement with Regard to Speaking in Tongues," the ALC, which had been affected first by the movement, denied that glossolalia is normative for Christian growth in grace and advised that the gift be used only for private devotion. A 1972 LCMS report, "The Charismatic Movement and Lutheran Theology," saw glossolalia as a gift limited to the early apostolic church and denied that the gift is a contemporary sign of God's grace. The LCA's 1974 report, "The Charismatic Movement in the LCA," recognized the charismatic movement as a legitimate part of the church's life and called for intensive study to help both insiders and outsiders deepen their experiences in accordance with Scripture and Lutheran theology.

The Division of Theological Studies, Lutheran Council in the USA, issued a report on "Evangelical, Liberation, and Charismatic Movements," prepared by the Institute for Ecumenical Research in 1975, which called the charismatic movement a challenge to Lutheranism's commitment to renewal and reform. The division encouraged study and critical discussion of the Lutheran charismatic movement through a series of conferences held at Wartburg Seminary in Dubuque, Iowa, in 1974. The conferences were attended by Lutheran charismatic leaders in addition to other participants, and resulted in the publication of essays on *The Holy Spirit in the Life of the Church.*[13]

The new charismatics, regardless of their denominational affiliation, are generally agreed that their movement should not become another denomination. Instead, they call for a greater expression of the emotional side of faith, an intensification of prayer, and the tolerance of special charisma such as glossolalia. Theologians in the movement argue that the church itself, indeed every Christian, is "charismatic" in the sense that baptism confers the Holy Spirit upon the individual. Clergy and laity from various denominations have been united through the new movement in such a way that genuine ecumenical encounter through study, prayer, and worship is furthered. There is evidence that the classic pentecostal demand for glossolalia as the decisive norm of the Christian life has disappeared in the new charismatic movement, even though speaking in tongues as an experience of a "second baptism" by the Holy Spirit is still a dominant form of testimony.[14]

CONVERGENCES AND DIVERGENCES

What does it mean to be "charismatic"? Every Christian is a charismatic, according to ancient New Testament tradition. For centuries, Eastern Orthodox Christians have insisted that the true aim of Christian life is the experiencing of the Holy Spirit, especially through initiation by baptism, chrismation (with holy oil, indidicating "confirmation"), and the Lord's Supper. In Eastern Orthodox churches, all three rites of initiation are performed together so that infant baptism, for example, is always accompanied by chrismation and Holy Communion. The Western church, represented by Roman Catholicism until the sixteenth-century Reformation, continued to link the experiencing of the Holy Spirit with the reception of sacraments, especially baptism, which emerged as the principal sacrament of initiation after the first millennium of Western Christian history.

Ancient traditions in both the East and the West have therefore not stressed a special experiencing of the Holy Spirit in the sense of "gifts" or "fruits" encountered by Paul in the Corinthian congregation (1 Corinthians 12). The fathers of the church, whether Origen in the East or Augustine in the West, regarded salvation as the work of God's grace which, through proper participation in the communication event of Word and sacrament, leads sinful creatures from cradle to grave. In this sense, salvation is conceived as a continuous process rather than an experience in delineated stages such as justification and sanctification.

Whereas specific charismatic gifts such as prophecy, healing, and speaking in tongues have always appeared in Christian history,[15] the emphasis on self-reflection and analysis of human experience became dominant during the eighteenth-century Enlightenment. The holiness revival, originating in Methodism, shared the classic Protestant "pietist" concern for sanctification: the embodiment of the gospel in a new, "converted" life demonstrating the distinction between worldly and pious living.

Pietism, a nickname associated with the defenders of sanctification in Germany, was a Lutheran renewal movement which began when Philipp J. Spener published a manifesto (*Pia desideria*, "pious desires") against Lutheran orthodox rationalists in 1675. The manifesto called for the correction of corrupt conditions in Lutheran state churches through Bible study, the revival of a lay ministry, and training in a practical Christianity concentrating on a new life rather than on new doctrines.[16] This call for what could be described as a religion of the heart, in opposition to a religion of the head (Lutheran orthodoxy had created the latter by concentrating on confessionalist doctrines after 1580) created a moral revival in Germany and provided the basis for educational and social reforms.

There is an emphasis on feeling both in the charismatic movement and in pietism; both use terms such as *rebirth, conversion, purity of heart* and the language of prayer and praise; both perceive God's incarnation in Christ in biological terms—the sinner's "regeneration" and "growth in grace." "It is by no means enough to have knowledge of Christian faith," Spener declared, "for Christianity consists rather of practice."[17] It is this concentration on sanctification which Methodism pursues in its doctrine of perfection.

The experience of Pentecost, consisting of speaking in tongues, was perceived to be the birth of the church as a missionary instrument. Those Methodists who looked for special evidence of the Holy Spirit in the face of denominational apathy found it in the gifts or fruits of the Holy Spirit. Pentecostal theologians usually speak of nine "gifts" and nine "fruits" of the Holy Spirit (mentioned in 1 Cor. 12:8–10 and Gal. 5:22–23). Whereas fruits designate the general regeneration of the individual believer expressed in a new stance of unselfish love, the gifts impart special power through baptism by the Holy Spirit. Thus speaking in tongues is not an odd event, but "a real necessity if a Christian is to have an unshakable certainty that the Spirit has truly and fully come to him."[18]

There is, then, a definite "order of salvation" in the pentecostal perception of the Christian life. First, Christ atones for the sins of humankind; then a new life begins, evidenced in a general conversion from selfish pride to unselfish love; and, finally, there is the personal certainty of salvation through baptism by the Holy Spirit.

What Wesleyan theology still regarded as a struggle between imperfection and perfection is seen in American pentecostalism as a steady growth from sanctification to perfection through the special assistance of the Holy Spirit. Christ's first work, justification, leads to his second work, sanctification, and climaxes in baptism by the Holy Spirit. Whereas there have been theological differences and controversies about the proper understanding of sanctification—whether Christ's work is finished, or whether baptism is by Jesus only and is to be followed by a second baptism by the Holy Spirit—those following the classical pentecostal tradition tend to think in perfectionist terms. Such thinking is frequently linked to an intensive anticipation of Christ's Second Coming, as in the Four-square Gospel Church.

On the whole, both traditional pentecostals and new charismatics tend to develop a rigorous ethical discipline in order to demonstrate the distinction between this world and the next. Thus charismatic experience leads to tithing, strict Sunday or Sabbath laws, pacifism, and restrictions on food and sex.

Roman Catholic, Anglican, and Lutheran charismatics also feel a need to move from justification to sanctification, from testifying to what God did in the crucifixion of Jesus to confessing how God's work in Christ affects personal lives. Some, no doubt, have joined the charismatic movement because they think there is no room in their churches for the joy of Christian experience. They are not eager to speak in tongues; they just want to express feelings and share experiences they think they have in common with other Christians.

Some heirs of the Protestant Reformation, however, especially Lutherans, suspect that almost any concern for the self and its security are acts of the devil, who has always wanted believers to worship themselves rather than God. Thus many Lutherans do not even want to talk about "spiritual experience" or "growth in grace."

In certain churches, there has always been a need to provide space for the language of joy and of Christian experience, even though it is understood that such behavior does not necessarily lead to self-righteousness. The Augsburg Confession describes the move from justifying faith to sanctified life:

> Faith is bound to bring forth good fruits and . . . it is necessary to do good works . . . because it is God's will and not because we place our trust in them as if thereby to merit favor before God.[19]

But the language of Christian experience becomes problematic when it is preoccupied with the self rather than with the other—the neighbor. Christian narcissism exists when the gospel about Jesus gets confused with the "good news" of how good one *feels* after conversion. When charismatics become preoccupied with religious feelings and with extraordinary experiences such as speaking in tongues, they have left Christianity's center of gravity, which celebrates the gifts of the Holy Spirit but does not use these gifts to determine who is or who is not saved.

NOTES

1. For a typical pentecostal account, see Klaude Kendrick, *The Promise Fulfilled: A History of the Modern Pentecostal Movement* (Springfield, Mo.: Gospel Publishing House, 1961), chaps. 2–3. A good scholarly treatment is Ronald A. Knox, *Enthusiasm: A Chapter in the History of Religion with Special Reference to the Seventeenth and Eighteenth Centuries* (New York: Oxford University Press, 1961), chap. 8. Knox also traces the link between Methodism and other revival movements.

2. Quoted in Nils Bloch-Hoell, *The Pentecostal Movement: Its Origin, Development, and Distinctive Character* (New York: Humanities Press, 1964), p. 23. A detailed account is also offered in Vinson Synan, *The Holiness–Pentecostal Movement in the United States* (Grand Rapids, Mich.: Wm. B. Eerdmans Publishing Co., 1971), chap. 5.

3. See the account in Bloch-Hoell, chaps. 4–5.

4. The text of "The Apostolic Faith Movement" is found in ibid., pp. 45–46, and in Walter J. Hollenweger, *The Pentecostals: The Charismatic Movement in the Churches*, trans. R. A. Wilson (Minneapolis: Augsburg Publishing House, 1972), p. 513.

5. Quoted in Kendrick, *Promise Fulfilled*, p. 155.

6. Quoted in Richard Quebedeaux, *The New Charismatics: The Origins, Development, and Significance of New-Pentecostalism* (Garden City, N.Y.: Doubleday & Co., 1976), p. 7.

7. For the full text of Michael Harper's platform, see ibid., pp. 104–105.

8. See chap. 3, with this title, in Kilian McDonnell, *Charismatic Renewal and the Churches* (New York: Seabury Press, 1976). McDonnell was the principal writer of the Roman Catholic *Theological and Pastoral Orientations on the Catholic Charismatic Renewal* (Malinas, Belgium, 1974).

9. See the brief account in Erling Jorstad, *Bold in the Spirit: Lutheran Charismatic Renewal in America Today* (Minneapolis: Augsburg Publishing House, 1974).

10. *Speaking in Tongues and Its Significance for the Church* (Minneapolis: Bethany Fellowship, 1968) is typical.

11. From their brochure, quoted in Jorstad, *Bold in the Spirit*, p. 95.

12. See "A Statement with Regard to Speaking in Tongues," *Reports and Actions of the Second General Convention of the American Lutheran Church*, 1964, Exhibit J, pp. 162–64, reprinted in Walter Wietzke and Jack Hustad, eds., *Towards a Mutual Understanding of Neo-Pentecostalism* (Minneapolis: Augsburg Publishing House, 1973), pp. 12–13. "The Charismatic Movement and Lutheran Theology," a Report of the Commission on Theology and Church Relations of The Lutheran Church–Missouri Synod, 1972. "The Charismatic Movement in the Lutheran Church in America," a paper by the Lutheran Church in America, 1974. "Evangelical, Liberation, and Charismatic Movements: Their Problem and Significance Within Ecclesiological and Ecumenical Frameworks," in *Studies* (Division of Theological Studies, Lutheran Council in the USA, statement by the Institute for Ecumenical Research, Strasbourg, France, 1978).

13. See Paul P. Opsahl, ed., *The Holy Spirit in the Life of the Church* (Minneapolis: Augsburg Publishing House, 1978).

14. See, for example, the periodical *Lutheran Renewal International*, which first appeared in 1980 as the voice of the International Lutheran Center for Church Renewal in St. Paul, Minnesota.

15. Hollenweger, *The Pentecostals*, surveys pentecostal phenomena in the United States, Brazil, South Africa, Britain, Germany, Italy, and Russia.

16. See "Proposals to Correct Conditions in the Church" in Philipp J. Spener, *Pia desideria*, trans. and ed. Theodore G. Tappert (Philadelphia: Fortress Press, 1964), pp. 87–122.

17. Ibid., p. 95.

18. See Dale F. Bruner, *A Theology of the Holy Spirit: The Pentecostal Experience and the New Testament* (Grand Rapids, Mich.: Wm. B. Eerdmans Publishing Co., 1970), p. 82. How pentecostal scholars are trying to wrestle with biblical authority is illustrated by Gordon D. Fee, "Hermeneutics and Historical Precedent—A Major Problem in Pentecostal Hermeneutics," in *Perspectives on the New Pentecostalism*, ed. Russell P. Spittler (Grand Rapids, Mich.: Baker Book House, 1976), pp. 119–32.

19. Article VI.1, "The New Obedience," in *The Book of Concord*, ed. Theodore G. Tappert (Philadelphia: Fortress Press, 1959), p. 33.

5

Born-Again Experience and Baptism

REBIRTH AND CONVERSION

Propagators of the born-again movement, be they millennialists, fundamentalists, or charismatics, describe the born-again experience as a radical change of life style. Popular born-again literature attempts to attract people by describing the process in psychological terms. A widely distributed pamphlet,[1] for example, first poses and then answers two questions: (1) What happens when you are born again? (2) How do you become born again?

The answer to the first question consists of five parts: (1) "Guilt is washed away." This is exemplified by an unwed mother who felt liberated when Christ entered her life through Bible study. (2) "A new source of strength and nourishment is now available." This is exhibited in the strength to say, "Yes, I can. God is with me." (3) "There is an awareness that your life is now purposeful." That is, there is an awareness of what God is doing in daily life. (4) "You are beginning a life of growth and maturation." This is the definition of biblical sanctification. (5) "You have God's Word available to feed, nurture and train you in living that will build up yourself."

The answer to the second question consists of seven parts: (1) "Acknowledge your sin." This requires brainwork, that is, concentrating on personal needs, on the inability to save oneself, and on one's dependence on God. A salesman tells how his conversion brought him peace from the pressures of business. (2) "Repent and forsake sin." This involves moving from feeling bad to a new way of thinking. A British couple tells how their conversion during a Billy Graham crusade in London changed their lives by removing from them the temptations of drinking, swearing, and lying, and by bringing them into a new relationship with others. (3) "Trust Jesus Christ—invite him into your life." This requires turning away from sin and toward the redeemer of sin, who responds to invitations. An elderly lady tells how she received Christ when she prayed quietly after attending a wedding. (4) "Surrender to God's will." This requires letting Christ take charge of one's life, as illustrated by the conversion story of the Western stars Roy Rogers and Dale Evans. (5) "Overcome suffering and problems." Trials and tribulations will not go away, but they should be seen as tests in Christian training. To born-again parents, for example, a terminally ill baby is a special gift of God. (6) "Experience God's customized care." (7) "Accept salvation now." Readers are advised to pray a prescribed "prayer of commitment" and to follow it with regular prayer, Bible study (beginning with the Gospels of John and Mark), contact with other believers, and the sharing of one's personal decision with someone else.

In born-again literature as well as in born-again meetings, the conversion experience is seldom linked with water baptism, even though baptism is mentioned, usually in connection with "baptism by the Holy Spirit." Those who feel born-again think of sacraments as matters of church polity rather than as essential elements of gospel communication; therefore, one can be born again and still maintain membership in mainline denominations with "catholic" sacramental liturgies, such as Episcopalian, Lutheran, and Presbyterian churches.

Born-again people consider sacraments *adiaphora*—things which make no difference in the process of salvation, which, at best, confirm the reality of conversion in a symbolic way. Thus, baptism of adults may be a powerful symbol of personal rebirth, but baptism is completely powerless when administered to infants. Born-again people think this ideological position is in conformity with the early Christian evidence in the New Testament, and they maintain the "evangelical" consensus that there is no real connection between conversion and baptism. Billy Graham, for example, is silent about baptism in his lengthy *How to Be Born Again*. He cites numerous biblical examples and passages but does not deal with the relationship between rebirth and baptism at all, which a correct reading of the Bible would demand.[2]

The practice of infant baptism cannot be derived from biblical evidence beyond a reasonable doubt, but there is solid evidence for the close relationship between baptism and conversion.[3] There is also a close connection between the Old Testament view of the "return" (*shubh*) of the covenant people of Israel to God and Jesus' call for repentance prophesied by John the Baptist in Mark 1:1–15. The earliest history of Christian life, the Acts of the Apostles, clearly indicates how conversion was integrated with baptism. After the mass conversion at Pentecost, Peter called for the baptism of those who had repented and had received the Holy Spirit (Acts 2:38); his mission to the Gentiles always involved penance and baptism (Acts 10:44–48); and the reception of the Holy Spirit is linked with conversion *and* baptism (Acts 19:1–7).

Although Paul could say Christ sent him to preach the gospel rather than to baptize (1 Cor. 1:17), he nevertheless understood baptism as the means by which the atoning death of Jesus is embodied in Christian life (Rom. 6:3–4). "You were washed," Paul told the Corinthians who were confused about baptism and life, "you were sanctified, you were justified in the name of the Lord Jesus Christ and in the Spirit of our God" (1 Cor. 6:11). The Letter to the Ephesians speaks of "one Lord, one faith, one baptism" (Eph. 4:5). And the early church lived by Jesus' mandate to baptize "all nations." (Matt. 28:19).

The Gospel of John, in the often-quoted story of the encounter between Jesus and Nicodemus (John 3:1–21), sees the link between conversion and baptism as the change from unbelief to faith. To be born from above means to move in a new direction, namely, to participate in the atonement of Christ whose death and resurrection are enacted by immersing the penitent into running water and saying "I baptize you in the name of the Father and of the Son and of the Holy Spirit." In this sense, baptism is the initiation of converted adults into the history of salvation (begun in Israel and fulfilled in Christ, the mediator of a "new Israel") and the promise of eternal fellowship with God. The emphasis is always on the death and resurrection of Jesus rather than on the individual's spiritual experience.

The Gospel of John, in particular, stresses the incorporation of the believer into the work of Christ's mission. Paul made the same point when he told the Corinthians, "we were all baptized into one body—Jews or Greeks, slaves or free" (1 Cor. 12:13). The body of Christ is the church, and members of that body are marked by baptism, the indelible seal of their rebirth. "We were buried therefore with him [Christ] by baptism into death, so that as Christ was raised from the dead by the glory of the Father, we too might walk in newness of life" (Rom. 6:4). As one theologian put it:

> There are one or two things that may be surely said without fear of contradiction. The first is that in the New Testament baptism always marks the incorporation of the individual within the body of Christ.... Further it seems clear that, as marking incorporation into the body of Christ, *baptism is inseparably connected with regeneration or being born again.*[4]

As members of the body of Christ, however, Christians share both the glory and the cross of Christ in accordance with the commandment, "Greater love has no man than this, that a man lay down his life for his friends" (John 15:13). To be born again does not guarantee an uninterrupted life of glory but rather the beginning of a struggle to be in but not of this world.

CHRISTIAN FORMATION

Christian life is formed and "normed" by baptism. Why? Because God so willed it and commanded through Christ, "Go and baptize." "He who believes and is baptized will be saved" (Matt. 28:19; Mark 16:16).

All of life is ruled either by ego power or by gospel power. Ego power is manifested in the enduring human desire to exercise unlimited control, "to be like God." Gospel power is disclosed in God's unconditional promise that in Christ we are reconciled and returned to never-ending fellowship with God. Infant baptism is the visible word through which gospel power is communicated, even though the infant is not conscious of it. The classical debate over the preeminence of infant or adult baptism has rotated around the question of whether or not faith should precede baptism. One side has argued that only a "believer's baptism" is mandated by the New Testament, while the other side has insisted that "infant baptism" truly embodies gospel power, that is, God's unconditional love for the sinner.

Must faith precede baptism, as is written in Mark 16:16, "He who believes and is baptized will be saved"? Yes, was the answer of sixteenth-century defenders of "believers' baptism." Luther, however, charged them with faulty reasoning:

> Were we to follow their reasoning we would have to be baptizing all the time. For I would take the verse, "Whoever believes" with me, and whenever I find a Christian who has fallen or is without faith, I would say that this man is without faith, so his baptism is fruitless; he must be baptized again. If he falls a second time, I would say, see, he has no faith, there must be something wrong about his first baptism. He will have to be baptized a third time, and so on and on. As often as he falls or there is doubt about his faith, I will say he doesn't believe, his baptism is defective. In short, he will have to be baptized over again so often that he never again falls or is without faith, if he is to do justice to the verse, "Whoever believes." Tell me, what Christian will then ever be sufficiently baptized or consider that his baptism is complete?[5]

Ecumenical realists agree with Luther that those who focus on faith alone become victims of ego power, because their self has become more important than God. Baptism is the uncomfortable and, at times, offensive reminder that my salvation must come from outside myself if it is to be really effective against the original sin of taking charge of my life without any interference. The "old Adam" is always tempted by the promise of the serpent, "you will be like God" (Gen. 3:5). But the "new Adam" knows, through God's audible and visible Word, that God in Christ is the outsider who joins the fray and promises to win the battle against sin, evil, and death. And those who follow Christ and who baptized me as an infant share in the promise that I too shall overcome original sin.

Once I am baptized, I can return to my baptism, the norm which forms my life. How do I return to baptism? The classic ecumenical answer has always been "by receiving again and again the promise of divine forgiveness through the word of absolution from a fellow Christian." Tradition has called this the act of penance, consisting of confession and absolution. Sixteenth-century reformers reaffirmed this tradition in various ways. Luther spoke of two parts in the act of penance. "The first is my work and act, when I lament my sin and desire comfort and restoration for my soul. The second is a work which God does, when he absolves me of my sins through a word placed in the mouth of a man." Philipp Melanchthon regarded penance as the "third sacrament" (along with baptism and the Lord's Supper), which ensures forgiveness of post-baptismal sin.[6] Just as I was baptized by someone else in a gospel enactment consisting of water and words, so do I receive the power of baptism again in the promise of forgiveness spoken by another person, either privately or publicly in the liturgy of public and private confession, usually with the laying on of hands.

Thus baptism and penance are related in a structure one could call "Christian formation" or "Christian nurture." In the Middle Ages, this structure was sacramental: certain liturgical acts determined Christian lives from cradle to grave, beginning with infant baptism and ending with the sacrament of extreme unction. Luther and other sixteenth-century reformers reduced the number of sacraments, yet Lutheran hymnals, for example, have always included "orders" for both public and private confession. In general, these, too, follow the medieval order of linking confession to the Lord's Supper, which, according to Luther, "is given as a daily food and sustenance so that our faith may refresh and strengthen itself and not weaken in the struggle but grow continually stronger."[7]

There are, of course, significant differences between the sixteenth century and modern American culture, for in the sixteenth century an infant was born into a Christian culture and was nurtured by nothing but Christian life and thinking. Today, however, there is no longer a uniform Christian culture. Instead, there is a religious pluralism that offers a variety of religious options, including agnosticism and apathy. Some churches still nurture their people with both Word and sacrament, but a strong emphasis on the Word alone in some Protestant churches has led to a maceration of sacramental life.

How, then, does one return to baptism when the liturgical practices of penance and the Lord's Supper are reduced to a minimum or have acquired a merely symbolic character? How can baptized infants be initiated into Christian life when its communal aspects are nearly destroyed by the onslaught of individualistic piety and burdened by the anxiety of whether or not one has proof of having been born again? What happens to "baptism into the death of Christ" in the context of an educational philosophy stressing "potential," "development," and psychological "readiness"? How does one move from such a "natural" pedagogy to sacramental nurture? How significant are Word and sacrament in Christian formation?

Worship and catechetics have been the cornerstone of Christian life in the Western churches. Initially, the sixteenth-century reform movement tried to steer a middle course between the medieval church's almost magical stress on sacramental life and a "theology of the Word" which frequently resulted in a radical decrease of sacramental practices. Luther reformed Christian life in Wittenberg through a careful combination of worship and catechetics, ever mindful of the best and brightest moments in the ecumenical tradition. Catechetical programs and liturgical practices were intended to inform each other in such a way as to avoid theological confusion and abuse. Accordingly, Luther kept the ancient liturgical tradition of daily public worship in matins and vespers, but balanced liturgical celebration with intensive Bible reading and catechetical preaching; he continued the custom of weekly celebration of the Lord's Supper, but reduced the practice of praying to dead saints, since such a liturgy increased superstition among the common folk; and he favored baptism by immersion as a way of symbolizing baptism into the death of Christ.[8]

The born-again movement, with its tendency to ignore sacraments, challenges this traditional thinking about the interrelationship between baptism and Christian formation. There is a dire need for a holistic witness which seeks a proper balance between Word and sacrament as well as between the individual and the community. Human relationships in everyday life must not be separated from the "holy" celebrations of the gospel in Word and sacraments; and worship must not be separated from Christian education. Sunday worship and Sunday school lead to Monday ministry.

MORALITY

How does one behave as a Christian in the world? Although answers to this question have always varied, some Christian groups have pressed hard for a consensus. For example, many Christians believe that the Ten Commandments are timelessly valid, even though it may be difficult to apply them to certain situations. Pollsters have discovered that more than eight out of every ten Americans (eighty-four percent) believe that the Ten Commandments are valid today. But "fewer than half (forty-two percent) can name at least five of the Ten Commandments."[9]

It is always difficult to move from the general to the specific; yet true lovers know that love goes for details rather than generalities. Therefore, assuming that Christians live by the Ten Commandments, how are they to be obeyed? What does it mean, for example, to obey the Fifth Commandment, "You shall not kill"? Avoid war and become a pacifist? Oppose capital punishment, abortion, hunting, medical experiments using animals, raising cattle for food? Become an ascetic vegetarian? Why do Jews obey some of the Ten Commandments differently from Christians—in their attitude toward the Sabbath, for example? To what degree do the Ten Commandments reflect a "culture" or a "situational ethic" rather than an ethic of divine principles? Is the First Commandment, "You shall have no other gods," an unconditional divine mandate? Do other commandments need to be interpreted within a specific cultural context—for example, stealing is theft of private property according to Luther's commentary on the Seventh Commandment.[10]

Some denominations, and especially organized born-again Christians, concern themselves with a distinction between "Christian" and "secular" morality, a distinction they assume exists in the Bible. They apply this distinction at times to moral and political life, usually out of an almost paranoid fear that America is being threatened by evil forces aimed at the eradication of our original "Bible-based civilization."[11] That is why some born-again Christians follow the tradition established in American evangelism of organizing during local, regional, and national elections in order to attain specific political goals. Some simply espouse a kind of moral renewal based on puritan values concerning sex and family, while others band together to save the nation from what they believe to be total moral disintegration. Aiming at a "moral majority" in government, political born-again organizations have launched expensive media crusades against politicians they regard as defenders of "secular humanism" in public schools, of sexual promiscuity in private and public life, and of "liberal" causes grounded in sheer paganism. Their leaders have created an "electronic church," consisting of a television audience which is accustomed to remote control worship and which is loyal to powerful media revivalists.[12]

One way to overcome the confusion over morals and political questions is to obey unconditionally those Christian leaders who tell their members what to believe and how to behave. Sociological studies have shown that "social strength and leniency do not seem to go together."[13] Thus, many members of mainline denominations join Christian groups that demand strict adherence to moral and political norms, with no debate of the pros and cons of any particular situation or issue. The result is often the defense of a "civil religion" which undergirds a capitalist culture by celebrating the virtues of family, country, monogamy, work, frugality, sobriety, and other aspects of a "Protestant ethic."[14] Although many rank-and-file members of the born-again movement defend the authoritarian "Protestant ethic," there have been some significant convergences between evangelicals and mainline denominations regarding the relationship between doctrine derived from the Bible and moral issues seen from a sociopolitical perspective. The evangelical Lausanne Covenant on Evangelism has called for a "Christian social responsibility" which moves from personal behavior to political strategy to obtain justice.[15] Moreover, there are groups of radical "left evangelicals" who are working with "Protestant liberals" for social justice both within and outside the United States.[16]

But the basic ecumenical question is not whether Christian moral life moves in accordance with uniform norms derived from the Bible, but whether the event called "baptism" decisively shapes Christian life in the world. How, then, is the move made from baptism to moral life in the world? Baptism has ordained me into a ministry which I exercise in whatever position I have in life. My ministry is grounded in the promise, offered in the word of absolution and in the sacrament of the Lord's Supper, that whatever I do is a consequence of my faith in God's promise rather than a condition I am fulfilling to earn God's forgiveness. I serve my neighbor not because I need emotional satisfaction or because I hope thereby to make peace with God. Rather, I engage in moral action because I am to care for God's creation and my fellow creatures; and

I am truly free to do so because such care has nothing to do with my salvation. I am saved through Christ, not through morality.

When Christian life is nurtured by the continual promise of God's unconditional love, it is liberated from the egocentricity which always asks, "What's in it for me?" Although I am never completely freed from such egocentricity, my freedom to care for my neighbor is nourished by the promise that before God morality does not matter at all. What matters is my faithful relationship to God, nurtured by Word and sacrament. I need this nurture because of the constant temptation to be proud of my morality rather than to be faithful in my discipleship to Christ.

This discipleship is embodied in the visible, existential gathering of Christians who, warts and all, assemble according to the gospel promise that "where two or three are gathered in my name, there am I in the midst of them" (Matt. 18:20). Neither obedient membership in a "moral majority" nor loyal adherence to the "electronic church" can substitute for the historical, visible gathering of the "body of Christ." There is no Christian life unless it is life in the gathered body of Christ, the church catholic, created and sustained by the "Word become flesh" (John 1:14).

When the norm of life is God's judgment in Christ, moral discourse and action become liberated from the ulterior egocentric motives which so easily infiltrate Christian minds and hearts. Grounded in the death of Christ and in love for the neighbor, Christians can be truly free to feed the hungry, care for the weak, or engage in political struggles for justice, simply because they truly care for the hungry and the oppressed. Thus, they may team up with all kinds of groups who seek equity and justice in a world plagued by inequality and injustice.

This does not mean that the church, for example, simply identifies with organizations that work for a better world. Believers know that they can cooperate despite all risks because they know that the coming of the Lord, not a political program, will ultimately make the difference. There is always the risk of "bold sinning," that is, the possibility that what appears good for the neighbor may instead turn out to be evil. Yet, having employed all their powers of human reason to discover what is best, Christians can proceed to do what they deem necessary. They will never build the kingdom of

God on earth, but they will be able to secure a measure of justice and thus provide a glimpse of the future promised by the gospel.

NOTES

1. See *Born Again: What Does It Really Mean?* (Fuller Evangelistic Association, Box 123, Los Angeles, Calif.).

2. See Billy Graham, *How to Be Born Again* (Waco, Tex.: Word Books, 1977), especially chap. 12.

3. See Paul Löffler, "The Biblical Concept of Conversion," in *Mission Trends No. 2: Evangelization*, ed. Gerald H. Anderson and Thomas F. Stransky (Grand Rapids, Mich.: Wm. B. Eerdmans Publishing Co., 1975), pp. 24–42. For the pros and cons of the origins of infant baptism, see Kurt Aland, *Did the Early Church Baptize Infants?* (Philadelphia: Westminster Press, 1963), and Joachim Jeremias, *The Origins of Infant Baptism* (London: SCM Press, 1963).

4. John Baillie, *Baptism and Conversion* (New York: Charles Scribner's Sons, 1963), pp. 16–17.

5. "Concerning Rebaptism," in *Luther's Works*, American Edition, vol. 40 (Philadelphia: Fortress Press, 1958), pp. 247–48.

6. Apology of the Augsburg Confession, 13:4, in *The Book of Concord*, ed. Theodore G. Tappert (Philadelphia: Fortress Press, 1959), p. 211. The Luther quotation is from the Large Catechism in *The Book of Concord*, pp. 458–459:15.

7. Large Catechism (Lord's Supper), in *The Book of Concord*, p. 449:24.

8. "Concerning the Order of Public Worship," in *Luther's Works*, American Edition, vol. 53 (Philadelphia: Fortress Press, 1965), pp. 12, 14, 100 n. 2.

9. *Christianity Today* (21 December 1979), p. 14.

10. "Large Catechism," in *The Book of Concord*, pp. 371:48, 395:223.

11. For the history of this fear, see George M. Marsden, *Fundamentalism and American Culture* (New York: Oxford University Press, 1980), chap. 23, "Fundamentalism as a Political Phenomenon."

12. How television has been used to promote the born-again movement has been shown by Jeffrey K. Hadden and Charles E. Swann, *Prime Time Preachers* (Reading, Mass.: Addison Wesley, 1981). A typical example of the combining of politics and the electronic church is Jerry Falwell, founder of the "Moral Majority," during the 1980 presidential election. See his manifesto, *Listen America* (New York: Doubleday & Co., 1980). See also the study of Lowell D. Streiker and Gerald S. Strober, *Religion and the*

New Majority: Billy Graham, Middle America and the Politics of the 70s (New York: Association Press, 1972).

13. See Dean M. Kelley, *Why Conservative Churches Are Growing,* 2d rev. ed. (New York: Harper & Row, 1977), p. 83.

14. A popular thesis proposed by Max Weber. See Robert W. Green, *Protestantism and Capitalism: The Weber Thesis and Its Critics* (Boston: D. C. Heath and Company, 1959).

15. Rene C. Padilla, *The New Face of Evangelicalism: An International Symposium on the Lausanne Covenant* (London: Hodder and Stoughton, 1976), p. 101.

16. See Richard Quebedeaux, *The Worldly Evangelicals* (New York: Harper & Row, 1978), chap. 10.

Conclusion

The born-again movement is part of a widespread dissent from the mainstream of American Protestantism which had become linked to popular ideals and patterns of American life: patriotism, manifest destiny, Anglo-Saxon self-confidence, the common folks' social and economic aspirations, and whatever the American dream and the Constitution promised. The dissent was propelled by agnostics, social gospelers, defenders of ethnic roots (blacks, Roman Catholics, Lutherans, and others who were not part of the old mainstream), and "evangelicals" who advocated a return to old-time religion. Speculations about the end time, biblical inerrancy, and a drive for holiness came to be the distinctive features of "evangelicals" so that "most Europeans regard them, along with baseball and wild-west movies, as American creations."[1]

If fundamentalism represents the perduring Christian temptation to capture the gospel in rational dogma, and the charismatic movement embodies the temptation to relegate the dynamic power of faith to special experience, then both movements are paradigmatic for Christian existence in the world. Rational dogma and emotional experience—the head and the heart—have always been the means employed by troubled consciences to find security and peace. It is comforting to *know* one is born again, through convincing rational arguments derived from the Bible as the inspired book of unerring divine truth. It is equally consoling to *feel* born again, through overwhelming emotional experiences caused by the unpredictable Holy Spirit who "blows where it wills" (John 3:8).

When the fundamentalist–charismatic desire for rational and emotional security is combined with speculations regarding the end time, especially millennialism, a powerful movement is born, intent on cleansing institutional Christianity from dangerous "secularizations," be they humanistic, communistic, Americanistic, or whatever. The born-again movement therefore represents the classic restitutionist ideal: to bring to life again the ancient, golden age of Christianity when sinful people were renewed by walking and talking with Jesus, who came to make the world ready for the kingdom of God in which sin, death, and evil would be no more.

The fundamentalist component of the born-again movement tends to combine its restitutionist ideal of an inerrant Bible with a longing for God that is so prevalent in the history of religions. Some of the best and brightest Christian minds have in the past been tempted to link religious longing for a God who fills all human gaps by being nonhuman, to the story of Jesus Christ. The apostle Paul, for example, was once desperate enough to tell the philosophers of Athens that the one they labeled the "unknown god" was in reality the Father of Jesus Christ, in whom they should believe (Acts 17:16–34). Legend has it that one of those who were converted by Paul's desperate sermon, Dionysius the Areopagite, became the founder of Christian mysticism. There has always been a kinship between rationalists and mystics because they desire to think or feel their way from bondage to the world to union with God. Like many medieval scholastics, best represented by Thomas Aquinas, fundamentalists assume that there is a mystical connection between faith and reason, leading to an other-worldly, supernatural relationship with God.

The charismatic component of the born-again movement bridges the gap between the first and second coming of Christ by the experiencing of an ahistorical conversion, frequently climaxing in xenolalia and glossolalia as signs of an emotional rapture (ascension) from the world of sin, death, and evil. Thus charismatics are "enthused," that is, they experience "being in God" (from the Greek *entheos*) without benefit of books or rational doctrines. The conversion experience is understood to be a foretaste of the future life with God. Charismatics often claim, as did the apostle Paul, that they are "caught up to the third heaven" not knowing "whether [they are] in the body or out of the body" (2 Cor. 12:2). But unlike Paul, charismatics tend to stress inward, spiritual joy rather than external, existential suffering in a world plagued by the powers of sin, death, and evil.

Frequently disenchanted with the lack of Christian cheer in the worship and life of the organized church, charismatics want to witness to the power of the Holy Spirit who brings the fruits of love, freedom, and joy. But although such witness may serve as an appropriate corrective to a penitential, puritan Christianity, it must never be forgotten that Christian life must embody the difference between the power of the ego, which tries to escape from suffering, and sacrificial love, the greatest of all "gifts of the Spirit" (1 Cor. 13:13).

To be truly born again means to lead a life of cruciform discipleship in the name of Jesus Christ, who was crucified and resurrected. Such discipleship is always endangered by the temptation "to do one's own thing" or "to be like God" (Gen. 3:5) rather than to deny oneself and bear the cross of obedience to death (Matt. 16:24–25). As long as they live in the world, Christians will always encounter both the way of the serpent and the way of the cross. Christian realism warns against relying on ego power in this encounter. "I can will what is right, but I cannot do it. For I do not do the good I want, but the evil I do not want is what I do" (Rom. 7:18b–19). That is why the life of the individual Christian constantly needs to be "re-formed" in partnership with others who, as the gathered body of Christ, speak to and enact with each other the good news that salvation comes from a God who died on the cross rather than from any human effort, offensive as such a gospel may be to those who desire a more elegant God or a greater reliance on their own pride.

The truly ecumenical question is not whether one has had that one, glorious, born-again experience, be it through Bible or Spirit or both, but rather whether one is born again and again in the encounter with the gospel of Christ crucified.

NOTES

1. Sidney E. Ahlstrom, *A Religious History of the American People* (New Haven: Yale University Press, 1972), p. 806. Chapter 48 describes this "dissent and reaction in Protestantism."

Suggested Readings

GENERAL

Ahlstrom, Sidney E. *A Religious History of the American People.* New Haven: Yale University Press, 1972. More than one thousand pages of history, stressing Puritan roots, with "evangelicalism" as a significant branch since the 1860s. Very helpful index and bibliography.

Cohn, Norman. *The Pursuit of the Millennium: Revolutionary Messianism in Medieval and Reformation Europe and Its Bearing on Modern Totalitarian Movements.* New York: Harper Torch Books, 1961. Good background reading for an understanding of the Judeo-Christian apocalyptic tradition, especially its Protestant component.

Hadden, Jeffrey K. and Swann, Charles E. *Primetime Preachers: The Rising Power of Televangelism.* Reading, Mass.: Addison Wesley, 1981. A useful guide through the maze of TV programs broadcasting "old time religion," with sketches of principal leaders of the born-again movement.

Kelly, Dean M. *Why Conservative Churches are Growing.* 2d rev. ed. New York: Harper & Row, 1977. Argues that strict doctrinal and ethical demands attract more people than do "liberal" or lenient religious platforms.

Knox, Ronald A. *Enthusiasm: A Chapter in the History of Religion with Special Reference to the Seventeenth and Eighteenth Centuries.* New York: Oxford University Press, 1961. Should be read as a continuation of Cohn's study of millennialism. A Roman Catholic treatment of revival movements including Quakers, Moravians, and Methodists who are forerunners of modern revivalism.

Mead, Sidney E. *The Lively Experiment: The Shaping of Christianity in America.* New York: Harper & Row, 1963. A basic survey stressing non-puritan Enlightenment roots, with "denominationalism" and "Americanism" as the most important features. Different from Ahlstrom in size and content.

Niebuhr, Richard H. *Christ and Culture.* New York: Harper & Row, 1951. A typology showing the influence of culture on Christianity throughout its history. Good background reading for an understanding of the born-again movement as a cultural phenomenon.

Piepkorn, Arthur C. *Profiles in Belief: The Religious Bodies of the United States and Canada.* Holiness and Pentecostal, vol. 3; Evangelicals, Fundamentalists and Other Christian Bodies, vol. 4. New York: Harper & Row, 1979. Good summary of institutionalized millennialism, fundamentalism, and the charismatic movements.

Proctor, William. *The Born-Again Christian Catalog: A Complete Sourcebook for Evangelicals.* Old Tappan, N.J.: Revell, 1979. Written for born-again Christians in search of anything from colleges to entertainment in America. Discloses the variety of organizations within the born-again movement.

CHAPTER 1

Bloch-Hoell, Nils. *The Pentecostal Movement: Its Origins, Development and Distinctive Character.* New York: Humanities Press, 1964. A critical but objective account by a Norwegian author who has worked through most of the available sources.

Kendrick, Klaude. *The Promise Fulfilled: A History of the Modern Pentecostal Movement.* Springfield, Mo.: Gospel Publishing House, 1961. A defensive history of the movement.

Sandeen, Ernest R. *The Roots of Fundamentalism: British and American Millenarianism 1800-1930.* Chicago: University of Chicago Press, 1970. An authoritative study arguing the thesis that millennial hope runs through the fundamentalist and holiness movements since the 1790s.

CHAPTERS 2 AND 3

Barr, James. *Fundamentalism.* London: SCM Press, 1977. A solid analysis by an Oxford Bible scholar who argues that fundamentalism is a "philosophy" rather than just an approach to the Bible. Good bibliography and index.

Dollar, George W. *A History of Fundamentalism in America.* Greenville, S.C.: Bob Jones University, 1973. A defense of militant fundamentalism, though with valuable descriptions of various leaders and groups, concentrating on the Baptists.

The Fundamentals. 12 vols. in 2. Chicago: Testimony Publishing Company, 1910-1915. The widely circulated series of essays defending "fundamentals"; financed by the two oil millionaires Lyman and Milton Stewart.

Furniss, Norman F. *The Fundamentalist Controversy, 1918-1931.* New

Haven: Yale University Press, 1954. An account of the controversy in the South, climaxing in the famous Scopes trial in 1925.

Jorstad, Erling. *The Politics of Doomsday: Fundamentalists of the Far Right.* Nashville: Abingdon Press, 1970. Fascinating study showing how fundamentalism is linked to reactionary politics.

_____. *The Politics of Moralism.* Minneapolis: Augsburg Publishing House, 1981. Traces relationships between conservative Christianity and conservative politics.

Marsden. George M. *Fundamentalism and American Culture, 1870–1925: The Shaping of 20th Century Evangelicals.* New York: Oxford University Press, 1980. A very good study of political fundamentalism.

Padilla, René C., ed. *The New Face of Evangelicalism: An International Symposium on the Lausanne Covenant.* London: Hodder and Stoughton, 1976. Essays by principal spokespersons of the "evangelical" movement, disclosing a new ecumenical spirit among evangelicals.

Pierard, Richard V. *The Unequal Yoke: Evangelical Christianity and Political Conservatism.* New York: J. B. Lippincott Company, 1970. A Baptist historian's assessment of the link between evangelicals and politics. He defends the link.

Quebedeaux, Richard. *The Worldly Evangelicals.* New York: Harper & Row, 1978. Sketches the shift of evangelical intellectuals from a conservative to a liberal stance, especially on sociopolitical issues. Lists pamphlets and periodicals. Good bibliography.

Rudnick, Milton L. *Fundamentalism and the Missouri Synod: A Historical Study of Their Interaction and Mutual Influence.* St. Louis: Concordia Publishing House, 1966. An interesting case study which argues that Lutheran biblical fundamentalism stems from seventeenth-century orthodoxy rather than from the American movement.

Russell, C. Allyn. *Voices of American Fundamentalism: Seven Biographical Studies.* Philadelphia: Westminster Press, 1976. A Boston University scholar, who is a Baptist, presents the classical figures.

Sandeen, Ernest R. *The Origins of Fundamentalism: Toward a Historical Interpretation.* Facet Books, Historical Series. Edited by Richard C. Wolf. Philadelphia: Fortress Press, 1968. A brief summary by an expert, with a discussion of research.

Streiker, Lowell D. and Strober, Gerald S. *Religion and the New Majority: Billy Graham, Middle America and the Politics of the 70s.* New York: Association Press, 1972. A vivid portrayal of the link between evangelicals and politics.

Wells, David F. and Woodbridge, John D., eds. *The Evangelicals: What They Believe, Who They Are, and Where They Are Going.* Nashville:

Abingdon Press, 1975. A collection of essays by various scholars. Good bibliography.

CHAPTERS 4 AND 5

Agrimson, Elmo, ed. *Gifts of the Spirit and the Body of Christ: Perspectives on the Charismatic Movement.* Minneapolis: Augsburg Publishing House, 1974. Essays on biblical, historical, and sociological aspects.

Baillie, John. *Baptism and Conversion.* New York: Charles Scribner's Sons, 1963. Shows how baptism, conversion, and penance are interrelated in the New Testament.

Bruner, Dale F. *A Theology of the Holy Spirit: The Pentecostal Experience in the New Testament.* Grand Rapids, Mich.: Wm. B. Eerdmans Publishing Co., 1970. A major scholarly attempt by a pentecostal theologian to show the biblical roots of "baptism by the Holy Spirit."

Falwell, Jerry. *Listen America.* New York: Doubleday & Co., 1980. The manifesto of the leader of the Moral Majority among born-again and other Christians. Discloses Americanist ideology and political moralism.

Graham, Billy. *How to Be Born Again.* Waco, Texas: Word Books, 1977. A superficial prescription for repentance and conversion though without any reference to baptism.

Hollenweger, Walter J. *The Pentecostals: The Charismatic Movement in the Churches.* Translated by R. A. Wilson. Minneapolis: Augsburg Publishing House, 1972. An extensive survey and discussion of pentecostalism in every part of the world by a German author. Appendix offers the pentecostal "Declaration of Faith."

Jorstad, Erling. *The Holy Spirit in Today's Church: A Handbook of the New Pentecostalism.* Nashville: Abingdon Press, 1973. A sketch of major charismatic theological claims which avoids taking sides.

_____. *Bold in the Spirit: Lutheran Charismatic Renewal in America Today.* Minneapolis: Augsburg Publishing House, 1974. A useful survey of the origins and claims of the Lutheran movement with the story of its leader, Larry Christenson.

McDonnell, Kilian. *Charismatic Renewal and the Churches.* New York: Seabury Press, 1976. A sociological analysis by a Roman Catholic scholar who summarizes all official responses to the charismatic movement by American denominations. Good bibliography.

_____, ed. *Presence, Power, Praise: Documents on the Charismatic Renewal.* 3 vols. Collegeville, Minn.: Liturgical Press, 1981. Excellent collection of sources from 1960 to 1980. Includes international documents.

Opsahl, Paul, ed. *The Holy Spirit in the Life of the Church.* Minneapolis: Augsburg Publishing House, 1978. Essays dealing with biblical, historical, and theological views of the Holy Spirit by Lutheran scholars, including charismatics.

Quebedeaux, Richard. *The New Charismatics: The Origins, Development and Significance of Neo-Pentecostalism.* New York: Doubleday & Co., 1976. Good details and insight by an expert who is a member of the United Church of Christ. Sketches of individual leaders.

Schweizer, Eduard. *The Holy Spirit.* Philadelphia: Fortress Press, 1980. A sober assessment of biblical evidence by a solid Swiss New Testament scholar.

Synan, Vinson. *The Holiness-Pentecostal Movement in the U.S.* Grand Rapids, Mich.: Wm. B. Eerdmans Publishing Co., 1971. An inside account and survey of existing pentecostal churches in the U.S.

Theological and Pastoral Orientations on the Catholic Charismatic Renewal. Malinas, Belgium, 1974. A semiofficial position paper sponsored by Cardinal Suenens, widely used in Roman Catholic circles. Argues for pastoral integration of Catholic charismatics.